6·99

Roman Britain

WITHDRAWN

6

2 9 OCT 2007

IN THE SAME SERIES

General Editors: Eric J. Evans and P. D. King

Roman Britain

David Shotter

London and New York

First published 1998
by Routledge
11 New Fetter Lane, London EC4P 4EE

Simultaneously published in the USA and Canada
by Routledge
29 West 35th Street, New York, NY 10001

Typeset in Bembo by Routledge
Printed and bound in Great Britain by Clays Ltd, St Ives, PLC

British Library Cataloguing in Publication Data
A catalogue record for this book is available from the British Library

Library of Congress Cataloguing in Publication Data
Shotter, D. C. A. (David Colin Arthur)
Roman Britain/David Shotter (Lancaster Pamphlets)
Includes bibliographical references
1. Great Britain–History–Roman period, 55B.C.–449A.D.
2.Romans–Great Britain–History. I. Title. II. Series.
DA145.S54   1998
936.203–dc21   98-6933

ISBN 0–415–16579–2

Contents

Foreword

Lancaster Pamphlets offer concise and up-to-date accounts of major historical topics, primarily for the help of students preparing for Advanced Level examinations, though they should also be of value to those pursuing introductory courses in universities and other institutions of higher education. Without being all-embracing, their aims are to bring some of the central themes or problems confronting students and teachers into sharper focus than the textbook writer can hope to do; to provide the reader with some of the results of recent research which the textbook may not embody; and to stimulate thought about the whole interpreation of the topic under discussion.

Acknowledgements

I am grateful to Penguin Books for allowing me to use sections of Tacitus' *Life of Agricola* taken from the translation by Harold Mattingly in the Penguin Classics series. Maps 1, 2, and 4 are redrawn after J.S. Wacher, *The Coming of Rome* (published by Routledge), maps 3 and 5 after D.C.A. Shotter, *The Roman Frontier in Britain* (published by Carnegie Publishing). My thanks are due too to Susan Waddington and Emma Dick of the History Department at Lancaster University for their help with the preparation of the manuscript.

Maps

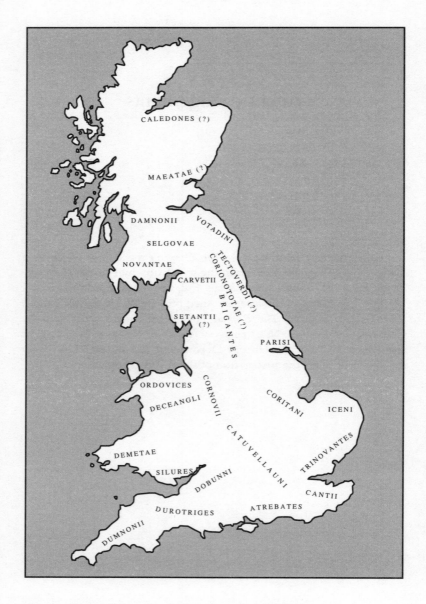

Map 1   Possible locations of tribes in pre–Roman Britain

Map 2   First stage of Roman conquest

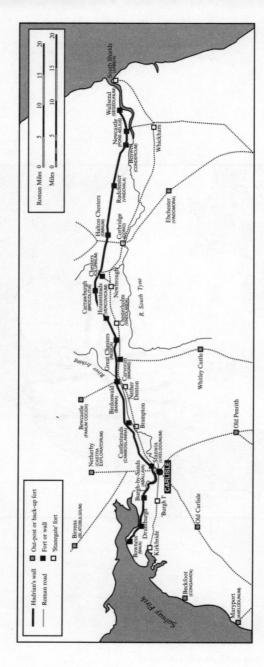

Map 3 Hadrian's Wall

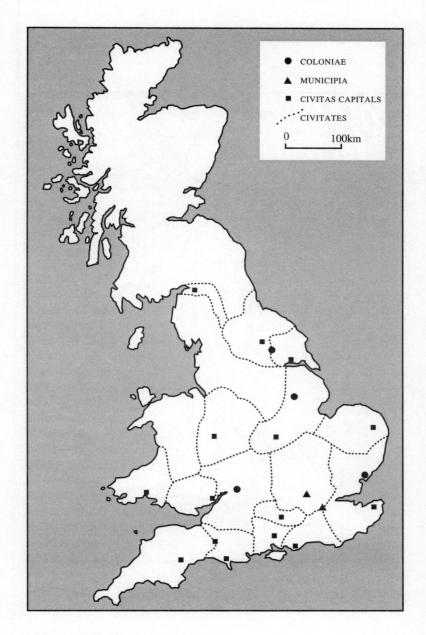

Map 4   Chief towns in Roman Britain

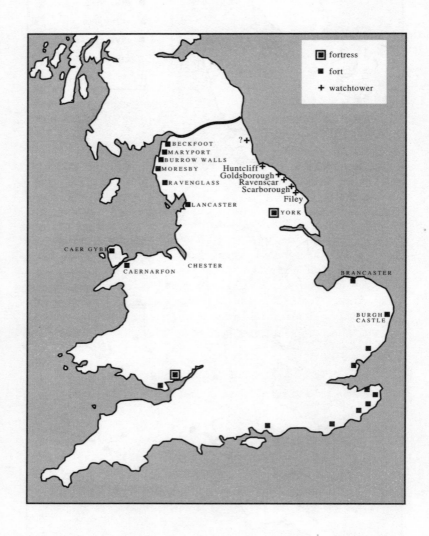

fortress
fort
watchtower

?

BECKFOOT
MARYPORT
BURROW WALLS
MORESBY
Huntcliff
Goldsborough
RAVENGLASS
Ravenscar
Scarborough
Filey
LANCASTER
YORK
CAER GYBI
CHESTER
BRANCASTER
CAERNARFON
BURGH
CASTLE

Map 5   Late Roman coastal defences

Introduction

Monty Python's *Life of Brian* posed the fundamental question, 'What did the Romans do for *us*?' Although flippantly posed in that context, the question has nonetheless exercised both scholars and non-specialists alike; a recent author put it in another way by seeing the Roman occupation as an 'interlude' in Celtic tribalism. It therefore seems reasonable to 'justify' the relevance of studying a period of British history so distant in time to a modern reader.

First, although population movements in the Iron-Age brought parts of Britain, culturally at least, into a wider frame, it was the Roman occupation that made Britain, in a structural sense, part of an organisation that comprised not just Europe, but also parts of the Middle East and north Africa. The active encouragement of the movement of people and goods within the Roman empire meant that Britain was subjected to a broader collection of cultural influences, and also had the chance to make its own impact. Britons served elsewhere in the empire and, as is shown by the 'Price Edict' of Diocletian (issued in AD 301), took the opportunity to sell their goods in the large market which the Roman empire represented. For a short time in the fourth century, as the 'Dark Age' was closing in on the European provinces, Britain was regarded as something of a haven, even an arsenal, for those trying to keep western Europe Roman. Thus, Britain was not simply a remote province on the far edge of the empire, but one which at times played a central role in the politics and economics of the empire – important enough to bring Roman emperors here in person.

1

Second, although Britain was physically remote from Rome, the structure of its society was fundamentally changed: Britons were not simply left as sullen spectators of the Roman occupation, but were encouraged into the business of administering their own provinces. Britons also benefited from the technological superiority of Rome: whilst more magnificent buildings were erected in other parts of the empire, the facilities which technology could provide were brought to Britain for the benefit of Britons who often depended upon investment which Roman financiers were prepared to make. Although argument can (and will) continue regarding the 'level of urbanisation' in Iron-Age Britain, there is no doubt that the Romans brought to Britain towns as we understand them. One of the difficulties in developing our knowledge of Romano-British towns is their very success. This led to the Roman levels being buried beneath the many centuries of developing townscape. Britain was not to see an equivalent level of technology until the late-seventeenth century.

Third, with the building of towns and forest clearance, the Roman occupation certainly altered the landscape of Britain in a permanent way. That landscape survives today in varied forms and its management is a recognised modern 'industry'. Because of the fascination exerted by surviving Roman remains in Britain, large numbers of people wish to become 'involved' in some way. Britain is probably unique in the way in which access to the heritage lies open for individuals and groups who are actively encouraged to participate in the processes of re-discovery and understanding. Discovery and the process of communication, therefore, not only 'feed' specialists in later periods of British history, but also create for the population at large – present and future – the ability to learn from, and to appreciate, the importance of the heritage. To do this successfully, however, each generation has to learn how to manage and care for what it has been bequeathed.

Finally, the study of Roman Britain is in no way a static and unchanging subject, new sites are constantly revealed, and new interpretative techniques deployed in understanding the subject. Many years ago, it was (accurately) observed that ultimately archaeology is about people. The people of Roman Britain reveal themselves through study – sometimes dramatically, as in the writing-tablets which were a chance discovery at the site of Vindolanda (in Northumberland). These tablets reveal people with surprisingly modern preoccupations – acquiring socks and underpants, going to parties. We also learn that a single day's pay for a legionary soldier

2

would buy 144 pints of beer! It comes as no surprise when military strength-lists from the same site indicate large numbers of soldiers on sick parade! Given the course of Britain's recent relations with Europe, there is a curiously modern ring to the tablet (of *c.* AD 100) which discloses that our Roman conquerors thought of us as 'nasty little Brits', incidentally providing us with a new Latin word coined for the purpose.

In such ways, the impact on Britain of the Roman occupation was considerable and reasearch provides, almost daily, new means of preventing such a study being dull or remote. If nothing else, the Romans have left us the opportunity to view the past not just through ruined buildings, but through their own eyes.

1

Rome and Britain

When Britain was finally annexed to the Roman empire in AD 43, conditions in the empire were very different to those at the time of Caesar's incursions a century before. The crucial difference was that the tottering and corrupt government of senate and people (the republic) had been swept away at the battle of Actium in 31 BC, and replaced by a form of monarchy, where central direction of imperial policy became possible. The historian, Tacitus, observed that the empire was the chief beneficiary of this change, gaining stability and sound government in place of corruption and exploitation.

During the republic, little thought had been given to the purpose of empire, and the addition of provinces had largely been incidental to warfare. Governors, who were members of the highly competitive senatorial aristocracy, in the main regarded provinces as sources of revenue to fund their patronage and electoral expenses; these were the keys to power in the republic. Alongside them was Rome's business community, members of the equestrian order, who undertook for profit – often excessive – the kinds of task, such as tax-collection and the management of state-property, which in a modern state would be the concern of a civil service. Although a mechanism existed by which provinces could seek redress against governmental malpractice (the 'extortion-court' or *quaestio de rebus repetundis*), access to it was difficult, and its decisions were often corrupted. In short, the comment on Roman imperialism placed by Tacitus in the mouth of the Caledonian chieftain, Calgacus, would have applied well to the

Roman attitude to the provinces in the republican period: 'They create a desolation, and call it peace.'

Even before the end of the republic, however, some things had begun to change: during his extended proconsulship in Gaul (58–50 BC), Julius Caesar clearly indicated directions for reform. His view that a purpose of empire was to provide a buffer between Rome and Italy on the one hand and dangerous and distant enemies on the other pointed in the direction of a 'frontier-policy' which could be achieved by the enhancement of natural features – for example, in western Europe, the river Rhine. Further, the fact that the Roman army (in Caesar's time, at least) did not make a particularly suitable garrison-force carried implications for the character of the administration of provinces; governors and tax-collectors needed to be subjected to tighter control, and if co-operation with provincials was to be secured, privileges of Roman citizenship had to be extended to those regarded as suitable; the tax-system had to reflect the need to leave sufficient wealth in the pockets of those whose co-operation was sought. In the empire, as in Rome, the authorities looked to rely on a system whereby the local upper classes undertook burdens at their own expense in return for political privileges.

Following the victory of Caesar's adopted son, Octavian (the future emperor Augustus), over Marcus Antonius in 31 BC, a clear opportunity – even necessity – existed to develop Caesar's thinking and to apply it more widely. Whilst a full discussion of Augustus' innovations is beyond the scope of the present chapter, a few observations are necessary to highlight the changes experienced by the provinces of the empire.

First, the nature of recruitment to, and service in, the Roman army was changed. The army, as before, was to consist of two types of troops. But the legions, who were Roman citizens, were now made fully professional and permanent by being given a 20-year term of engagement; they served alongside smaller units of infantry and cavalry, called 'auxiliaries' (*auxilia*), who were not Roman citizens and who 'signed on' for 25 years. These reforms allowed the army to be used not just for campaigning purposes, but for defensive and garrison-duties as well. This army swore an oath of allegiance to the emperor as its general (*imperator*), and in a sense represented the military backing which guaranteed his political security. As it would have been both offensive and counter-productive to have kept an army of 28 legions and an equivalent number of auxiliaries (approximately 300,000 troops) in close proximity to

5

Rome, it was obviously ideal to be able to disperse them to strategic points in the provinces.

The provinces themselves were divided into two types; those which were thought to require a military presence are termed 'imperial', whilst the rest are called 'senatorial'. In essence, the emperor was legally the *proconsul* of the first group, whilst in the latter the old practice of choosing governors by lot was maintained. An essential feature of the principate was the control exercised by the emperor over the election of state officials ('magistrates') from the senatorial order; this meant that by and large he approved of those who were elected. In imperial provinces, the emperor delegated his proconsular authority to an ex-magistrate, and was thus able to exercise choice and judgement over the matter directly. Such a man was then the *de facto* governor of the province, usually for a term of up to three years, and – a departure from republican practice – received a salary whilst in post. A poor performance on a governor's part would definitely affect future career prospects, and most emperors took considerable care to choose governors who would be efficient, loyal and beyond corruption. Although the emperor did not choose the governors of senatorial provinces, he could influence the choice and eliminate from the lot those whose appointments might be unsafe. From the time of Claudius (AD 41–54), it was normal for *all governors* to regard themselves as in the emperor's service.

The financial side of imperial administration was also overhauled. Imperial appointees from the equestrian order were placed in all provinces; these *procurators* were responsible to the emperor for such matters as tax-collection and the management of state property (such as grain-supplies and mines), and had under them junior officials who were also called *procurators*. In this way, although financial corruption was not totally banished, all provinces could expect a much more even and fair quality of financial administration. At first, at least, governors were evidently unable to interfere in the department of the *procurator*, though Tacitus records that in Britain Agricola (governor, AD 77–83) did act to check abuses of the tax-system; it is possible that this facility was introduced in the wake of the *procuratorial* improprieties which had precipitated Boudicca's rebellion in the province (see Chapter 2).

The centralised administration put in place by Augustus also meant that a 'philosophy of empire' could more readily be put into effect. As we have seen, Julius Caesar saw the empire as providing a protection from the enemies that Rome feared – particularly, the

German tribes who lived east of the Rhine, and the Parthians beyond the Tigris and Euphrates. The fears generated by these peoples were considerable; in the late republican period (in 54 and 36 BC) legionary standards ('eagles') were twice lost to the Parthians, and it took a considerable exercise of diplomacy on Augustus' part to achieve their return. Thereafter, a broad understanding existed between Rome and Parthia on the need for agreement on the chief bone of contention between them – who should rule in the kingdom of Armenia, which effectively constituted the 'buffer' between the two powers. Nonetheless, crises were not uncommon in the area – for example, when Trajan (AD 98–117) instituted large-scale plans for conquest and probably precipitated difficulties elsewhere in the empire by diverting troops to the area. This may have lain behind the evident instability in Britain that preceded the building of Hadrian's Wall. There was always the threat, therefore, that carefully contrived balances in other areas would be disturbed by the need to respond quickly to an upsurge of difficulty in sensitive theatres.

The dangers in Europe were highlighted by the loss of three entire legions east of the Rhine in AD 9; this disaster left on the Roman consciousness a constant fear of the uncontrollable power that lay in central and Eastern Europe. It was probably this that, in part, prompted the historian, Tacitus, to produce in AD 98 – the same year that saw the publication of his *Life of Agricola* – a treatise on the German tribes, normally entitled *Germania*. Although Augustus was probably looking to establish a frontier as far east as the river Elbe, he settled in the end for one which separated Romans and barbarians by means of the rivers Rhine and Danube; on his deathbed in AD 14, he issued to his successors the warning that the empire should be held within its existing boundaries. Thus, to the west and south of these lines provinces (or military districts) and client kingdoms were established to speed the process of Romanisation, whilst units of the army (legions and auxiliaries) were put in place at intervals to defend the frontiers from outside attack and to look inwards as defence-forces and in the role of a 'pioneer corps'.

The 'weak-point' in the European frontier – the 'gap' between the head-waters of the Rhine and Danube – was closed off with a complex of fortifications including roads, forts, turrets, ditches and palisades, strongly reminiscent of those which were being put in place between the Tyne and Solway at the turn of the first and second centuries AD. The care that the Romans took with this

'European frontier' was amply justified as the pressure built up along it from the late-first century, eventually of course becoming unstoppable. Again, the decision to invade Britain in the first place was, at least in part, related to the need to maintain the territorial integrity of this 'buffer' of territory to the west and south of the Rhine and the Danube.

As we have seen, it was politically dangerous and economically unacceptable to keep an unlimited number of men under arms; thus, co-operation with local people had to play an important role in making the 'buffer' effective. It is significant that the old republican notions of the empire being a field in which the senatorial aristocracy could win military glory was modified in the *Pax Romana* of Augustus; the 'new view' was aptly summarised by Virgil in his epic poem, the *Aeneid* (VI. 853):

> Your task, Roman, and do not forget it, will be to govern the peoples of the world in your empire. These will be your arts – and to impose a settled pattern upon peace, to pardon the defeated and war down the proud.

Chauvinism had given way to something which was, outwardly at least, more respectable: a mission to bring civilisation to the world.

The broad concept did not change greatly until the third century; the number of legions across the empire remained in the region of 28–30, although obviously, as Romanisation developed, the catchment area for the recruitment of Roman citizens into the legions broadened too. The auxiliaries, who in Augustus' time had been mostly local groups under their own commanders, were more obviously integrated into the army-structure. The 'ethnic exclusiveness' of units was probably watered down by local recruiting, and in time units of Britons were enrolled amongst the auxiliaries. The command-structure, too, was tightened, with officers of auxiliary units being drawn from Romanised personnel of equestrian (or 'middle-class') status. By the early second century AD, the auxiliary units, through Romanisation, had become increasingly similar to the legions, and Hadrian (AD 117–138) began to recruit so-called 'irregulars', mostly from frontier-areas. These were clearly meant to restore the novelty and dynamism originally provided by the auxiliaries. Such units can be recognised from a variety of titles; whereas auxiliaries were entitled *cohortes* (infantry cohorts) or *alae* (cavalry-wings), the irregulars bore titles, such as *milites* (soldiers), *pedites* (infantry), *equites* (cavalrymen), *numeri* (bands), or *cunei* (formations). Many such units can be recognised in Britain in the fourth century (listed in the *Notitia Dignitatum*), and they appear to have formed a significant part of the frontier-army of that period. We are also told by the historian, Dio Cassius, that after the Danubian wars of Marcus Aurelius (AD 161–180), some 5,000 Sarmatians were sent to Britain, although only one unit of them has ever been positively located – at Ribchester (Lancashire).

Romanisation also proceeded apace, with grants of citizenship allowing an increasing number of provincials to take some responsibility for conducting their own local affairs, and thus enabling administrative personnel 'from the centre' to be kept at relatively low and thus economical levels. Peace, of course, allowed the development of communications and the enhancement of trade and commerce; in this way, and through the tax-system, local individuals and communities could be enabled to increase their wealth. Growing prosperity facilitated faster progress in Romanisation and also allowed individuals with ambition to look to career-opportunities in the service of the central government. Thus, by the early third century the origins of more than half of the known senators in Rome lay in the provinces. Of these, Italy and the western provinces were the source of only 13.6 per cent in *c.* 220 (as compared with more than 75 per cent in the late first century AD), whereas the east provided 57.6 per cent, Africa 26.4 per cent and Illyria 2.4 per cent. Such developments need to be taken seriously into account when assessing the propriety of the criticism of Agricola's opponent, Calgacus.

Conditions and preoccupations in the later empire changed, and the empire's administrative system was radically overhauled by Diocletian to take account of this fact. The result was an increased (and increasing) bureaucracy, though no dramatic decline in prosperity can be detected until relatively late in the fourth century. These changes will be discussed more fully below, as they affected Britain.

Until its conquest by Rome in the first century AD, Britain continued to exert an air of mystery – the offshore island encountered after leaving the known world and embarking upon the 'ocean'. Many will have doubted whether it really existed. However, Britain had been encountered by Carthaginians and Greeks at least as early as the fourth century BC, as they explored and looked for new resources to tap. Archaeological evidence suggests a number of possible landfalls on the southern coast of Britain. In the second century BC, the activities of traders increased from southern Europe, through Gaul, and thence to Britain; particularly important here were connections between Britain's south-west peninsula and the Veneti of Brittany. Despite this, for Romans themselves Britain was of little concern prior to Julius Caesar's incursions in 55 and 54 BC.

Archaeologically, it is customary to think of Britain in both the pre-Roman Iron Age and during the Roman period itself as consisting of a Lowland and Highland zone, separated by a notional line drawn from north Yorkshire to the estuary of the river Dee (in Cheshire). South and east of this line, contacts with the Hallstatt and La Tène cultures of Iron-Age Europe are regarded as important, with 'invasions' of an Arras-related culture in the east, which manifested itself in the characteristic 'cart-burials' of its chieftains. North of the 'line', the people were culturally more primitive, although incursions from further south probably led, as there, to some tribal divisions and the beginnings of a political organisation. It is likely that as forest clearance proceeded, hierarchies arose based upon economic success and the ability to dominate through the production of a surplus which others needed.

The political shape of the Lowland zone began to develop during the second century BC, as the movements first of people in northern and central Europe and then of the Romans themselves started to precipitate westward migrations. The movements which necessitated the 'saving of Italy' by Gaius Marius in the late second century BC and Julius Caesar's Gallic invasions brought European tribesmen to join people in Britain who were often their kith and kin. Such people were relatively sophisticated in political organisation, commerce and industry; they were coin-using and had the use of the potter's wheel, manufacturing pottery which imitated familiar Roman types. Some had defensive sites on hill-tops, whilst others had already come down from the hills on to flat, quasi-urban, Lowland sites, as at St Albans, Chichester and Colchester. Their leaders maintained a dominance through patronage and through the enhancement of their wealth by means of agricultural enterprise, which, according to the Greek geographer Strabo, left them sufficient grain to export across to the continent of Europe. In both the north and the south, by the time that the Romans came, the British tribes enjoyed a leadership that was wealthy, astute, entrepreneurial – and effective.

Julius Caesar's activities in Gaul, which aimed at total conquest in western Europe, brought new people to Britain; this made Britain, in addition to its existing links with Europe, more significant to the security of Caesar's activities and, most importantly, his prospects of success in Gaul. Such was Caesar's position in Roman politics that he needed the wealth, reputation and military loyalty that success would bring. The 20 days of celebration decreed by the Roman senate following Caesar's incursions into Britain, whatever *their* view of Caesar's achievement, indicate that by *his* criteria he had won success. Yet, Caesar did not really bring Britain much closer to Rome; a century later, the embarking of an invasion force was almost as daunting an undertaking as it had been in 55 and 54 BC. Caesar's experience of Britain added relatively little knowledge to that which was available in the works which he probably used himself – those of the traveller Pytheas, from Marseilles, and of the philosopher and ethnographer, Posidonius of Rhodes (respectively late fourth and early first centuries BC).

The high profile of Caesar's incursions into Britain was due more to Caesar's position in Roman politics than to the quality of his achievement in Britain. Whilst he may have served his immediate purpose – of keeping the Britons of the south-east from interfering in Gaul – he made no permanent mark on Britain's political geography, nor did he significantly advance Rome's relations with Britain. Nor have Caesar's campaigns – a reconnaissance in 55 and an invasion in 54 – left any discernible mark on the British landscape, although some south-eastern hill-forts *may* reveal signs of resistance to Caesar.

Caesar's campaigning encompassed areas in south and south-eastern Britain, and extended as far north as a crossing of the river Thames. Although his chief British opponent, Cassivellaunus of the Catuvellauni, eventually surrendered to him, it was not before he had shown how difficult things could be made for a Roman leader by a tribal leader capable of uniting – even if only temporarily – anti-Roman forces. The strategy of 'divide and rule', which generally served Rome so well, showed weakness on this occasion. Together with this, Caesar was plagued by bad weather and by difficulties with the tides (which he had not properly investigated beforehand).

Visible success was vital, as Caesar's political enemies in Rome were clamouring for his recall from Gaul on the grounds of various illegalities committed both in Rome and in Gaul. Thus, Cassivellaunus' surrender was a great relief; it enabled Caesar to present his achievement as positive, and it facilitated his claim to have made Britain part of the empire. It also allowed him to initiate diplomatic moves in Britain which were aimed at creating tensions and balances between tribes in the south-east and were successful in preventing the tribal leaders interfering in Gaul as the process of stabilising Roman rule there got underway.

As Tacitus said, therefore:

> the deified Julius was the first Roman to attack Britain with an army, and although he frightened the natives by winning battles and established himself in coastal regions, it is now clear that his achievement was not the conquest of Britain, but an indication of how it might be done.
>
> (*Life of Agricola* 13)

2

The Roman conquest of Britain

The century that elapsed between Caesar's incursions and Claudius' invasion saw many changes in the relationship between Rome and the British tribes, largely based upon the inescapable fact that neither side could now afford to ignore the other. Rome wanted at least a balance of pro- and anti-Roman forces in southern Britain, if for no other reason than to retain conditions which would allow unimpeded progress towards Romanisation in Gaul.

In the immediate decades after Caesar's visits, tribal politics in Britain appear to have stabilised, and although pro- and anti-Roman stances were detectable, it made little immediate difference to the state of relations between Rome and the southern British tribes. Indeed, British tribes did business with Roman Gaul and, according to Strabo, commodities passing from Britain included grain. (The implications of this for the development of British agriculture are discussed in Chapter 5.) By the time that Augustus died in AD 14, the principal tribal groups were the Catuvellauni (north of the Thames) and the Atrebates (on the southern side of the river).

Of these, the Atrebates, although deriving from a Gallic tribe which had opposed Caesar, were the more firmly pro-Roman, whilst the Catuvellauni, who had effectively broken their agreement with Caesar that they would not interfere with their eastern neighbours, the Trinovantes, were antagonistic but circumspect. Both were effectively led – the Atrebates by Verica, who was a client of Rome and had principal centres at Silchester and Selsey, and the Catuvellauni by

Cunobelinus who ruled from Colchester and who, despite his independence of spirit, used coinage with the title, REX (King) and probably also enjoyed a treaty with Rome. The stances of the tribes was well caught by the symbolism of their coinage; Verica, indicating his sympathies and his commercial contacts with the Mediterranean, coined with a vine-leaf motif, whilst Cunobelinus coined with a prominent ear of barley – a 'trade-war' between Mediterranean wine and British beer!

At the beginning of his reign in 31 BC, Augustus had an invasion of Britain high on his agenda; the court-poet, Horace (Quintus Horatius Flaccus) had announced that Augustus would be considered a 'god upon earth' if he added the British to the Roman empire and a later historian, Dio Cassius, indicates that expeditions were planned in 27 and 26 BC. Augustus, as his reign developed, became increasingly pre-occupied with territorial wars in central Europe, which culminated in the major disaster in the Teutoburgerwald in AD 9, in which three complete legions were annihilated. It was undoubtedly within the more sober atmosphere that prevailed after this that Augustus is said to have advised his successor, Tiberius (AD 14–37), not to contemplate wars for territorial gain.

Tiberius, as always, took Augustus' advice, and no further moves were undertaken with regard to Britain. In general, British leaders appear to have remained co-operative, and we learn that in AD 16, when a number of Roman soldiers from the Rhine were swept by bad weather across the North Sea, they were returned to Rome by an unnamed British king – probably Cunobelinus. However, a hint that the quiescence of Britain could not be taken for granted is perhaps given by a serious outbreak of trouble in Gaul in AD 21 and 22, which appears to have been inspired by Druidic priests/military leaders; Tiberius is on record as having expelled Druids from Gaul.

Tiberius was succeeded in AD 37 by his great-nephew, Gaius Caligula (AD 37–41); this was a crucial time for Rome's relations with Britain, as both the long-standing leaders, Cunobelinus and Verica, were getting older and susceptible to more vigorous pressures. Cunobelinus must have died in *c.* AD 39, and his heirs were his three sons, Caratacus, Togodumnus and Adminius. Of these, the first two were spiritedly anti-Roman, whilst Adminius, perhaps to protect his inheritance, sought help from Rome and crossed the Channel to meet Caligula. It is in this context that we should view the 'British policy' of Caligula, which earned the universal contempt of surviving Roman writers; they saw it as an episode full of bizarre incidents and

14

inconsistencies which served to demonstrate the emperor's mental imbalance.

Caligula, however, was probably not ready in AD 40 to invade Britain; he did not trust members of the senatorial order whom he would have had to leave temporarily to their own devices and, more seriously, in the previous year he had had to act quickly to snuff out an incipient rebellion amongst some of the Rhine legions which left them in a demoralised state. The famous story that Caligula lined up his troops on the Gallic coast and gave them orders to gather sea-shells as 'the spoils of the Ocean' has been taken by most as a sign of the emperor's insanity. However, the story may have been a misunderstanding of (or a malicious invention based upon) formalities associated with the acceptance by Caligula of the submission of Adminius. The events may also have been intended as a timely warning to Adminius' brothers that Roman legions were not far away.

Caligula's successor, his uncle, Claudius (AD 41–54), brought to the 'British question' some different considerations from those that had exercised his predecessor. Whatever the precise circumstances of Caligula's death and Claudius' accession, a significant part had been played by officers and men of the praetorian guard; this may have impressed upon Claudius, who had little experience of public affairs and none of military matters, the need to project a more military image. Military conquest and the annexation of a new province were clearly powerful ways of achieving this. There was also, however, another dimension to Claudius' difficulties with the military which could be solved in the same way. There was great antagonism between the legionary army and the praetorian guard, who were regarded by the legionaries as effete, over-privileged and over-paid. As the protégé of the guard, Claudius risked aggravating legionary sensibilities; such a campaign as was contemplated in Britain would help to soothe these. Claudius had already had a warning of the potential danger, when in AD 42 the governor of a Danubian province had attempted to entice his legions to desert Claudius. In addition, the conquest of Britain would enhance Claudius' reputation and counter the widespread view that he was a fool.

Claudius suffered from physical disabilities which had prevented earlier emperors from wanting to use his services; consequently he had spent much more time in study than was normal for a Roman noble. As a student and writer of history Claudius probably had a better developed idea of Rome's 'mission' than most of his class. In

15

his administration in Rome, Claudius was to demonstrate that he was a radical thinker; in his view of empire he clearly was greatly taken by the example of Julius Caesar in terms of both imperial objectives and the means of achieving them. He more than most may have seen Britain as Caesar's 'unfinished business'.

It is clear from Tacitus' views on British geography that Romans saw Britain as more closely integrated into Europe than we might; it was envisaged as 'sitting in' a western European 'bay', so that a close relationship was thought to exist between Scots and Germans, English and Gauls, and Irish and Spanish. Such a view undoubtedly influenced the formulation of military imperatives. Finally, we should relate such considerations as these to the situation in Britain, where Roman interests were increasingly under threat. Caratacus and Togodumnus had demanded their brother's return and had set out on a policy of imperial aggrandisement, which had led them to take over parts at least of Verica's kingdom; this 'friend and ally of the Roman people' had been driven out, and undoubtedly wanted Rome to honour its side of their treaty. Further, the prospect of southern Britain united under hostile rulers, posed great dangers to Romanised Gaul. In short, all considerations pointed in the same direction: the time was ripe for Roman conquest.

The invasion force of AD 43 was formidable: four legions – II *Augusta*, IX *Hispana*, XIV *Gemina Martia Victrix* and XX *Valeria Victrix* – and, it seems, detachments (*vexillationes*) of others, together with an equivalent number of auxiliary troops; in all, a total force of around 45,000 men. It was led by Aulus Plautius, a senior senator in the emperor's service. The force landed at Richborough in late summer, in the first year defeated the British near the Medway, and went on to establish a legionary base at Colchester, Cunobelinus' old capital. Claudius himself joined his victorious army for the ceremonial entry. The high profile of the expedition is demonstrated by Claudius' decision to revive the antique ceremony of formally extending the city-limits of Rome, to construct triumphal arches both in Rome and Colchester and to issue commemorative coins.

From this 'bridgehead' the invasion essentially proceeded by three routes – northwards (along the line of Ermine Street) towards Lincoln, north-westwards (along the line of Watling Street) towards Wroxeter, and south-westwards (along the line of Stane Street) towards Exeter and into the territory of the Dobunni and the Durotriges. The precise courses are hard to check as the campaign-camps, each of which consisted of a bank and ditch enclosing an area for tents, have proved, as earth-work sites, notoriously vulnerable to centuries of plough-damage. Some indication, however, of the scope of early occupation is given by the distribution of forts of various sizes and vexillation-fortresses (for legionary detachments). Forts and fortresses assumed the characteristic shape – rectangular and with rounded corners.

Little is known in detail about the individual advance-routes, though the campaigns through the south and south-west must have been the most important in view of the fact that this was the direction taken by Caratacus after his initial defeat. This campaign was undertaken by II *Augusta*, which was at this time commanded by the future emperor, Vespasian; Suetonius, in his *Life of Vespasian*, indicates that successes included the capture of the Isle of Wight, the defeat of two tribes (presumably the Durotriges and the Dobunni), and the storming of more than 20 hill-forts. Two of these, Hod Hill and Maiden Castle, have provided dramatic evidence of the fighting and indicate the ferocity involved. Further, rather unusually, a Roman fort was established within the ramparts at Hod Hill, presumably to prevent its re-use. Normally, Roman forts were distinguished from their predecessors by being set in valleys on routes of communication.

Within a short time, the 'bridgehead' had grown to an area bounded approximately by the Fosse Way (Lincoln to Exeter) and policed throughout by a network of legionary fortresses and auxiliary forts. The Fosse Way itself, however, was not so much a frontier as a fortified route of lateral communication; there was no intention to halt the conquest on that line. A provincial administration was put in place to make progress with Romanisation, though some areas were left temporarily under local control; for example, Verica's successor, Cogidubnus, was given charge of a large area of Atrebatic territory based upon a new centre at Chichester, whilst in East Anglia, Prasutagus was entrusted with continued control of the Iceni. There was also a very significant treaty with 'queen' Cartimandua of the Brigantes (of northern England); by protecting Cartimandua from her factional opponents (principally her husband, Venutius), Rome hoped that stability on the north flank of the new province would facilitate the extension of the conquest into Wales, to where Caratacus had retreated after his defeat at Maiden Castle in Dorset.

Throughout the account of the conquest, the accuracy with which we can plot routes of advance and areas of campaigning is severely hampered by the poor quality of surviving information;

Roman authors, such as Tacitus who recounts periods of campaigning both in his *Life of Agricola* and his *Annals*, had little interest in facilitating the process of following routes 'on a map' or in reciting lists of place-names which would have meant little to a contemporary Roman audience. Such an audience wanted to know about morale, heroism, military vigour and persistence; locational information was useful only in so far as it enhanced the communication of human endeavour. This *lacuna* can be made good only gradually, as sites are discovered on the ground or from the air, as artefactual evidence places them in the relevant period(s) – or rules them out – and as the new sites are related (where appropriate) to ancient topographical descriptions. These are slow and necessarily imperfect processes; thus a true grasp of conquest and occupation is inevitably a long-term aim.

It was Caratacus who first drew the Romans into South Wales, where they may have employed a tactic later put to good use in northern England and Scotland – that of marching some troops overland and disembarking others from transport-ships (of the *classis Britannica*) at relevant points where they could join up with their colleagues. This tactic was intended to harass and 'squeeze' tribal armies in order to force the opposition to offer battle. The events which led up to Agricola's final battle against the Caledonians in AD 83 at *Mons Graupius* provides a notable example of this.

According to Tacitus, Caratacus used to the full his advantage of local knowledge and emphasised this when he retired from South Wales to make a final stand in the more difficult terrain of the north. In effect, however, he was allowing himself to be cornered, as the late 40s and early 50s saw the development of a line of legionary vexillation-fortresses (such as Rhyn Park, near Oswestry), which represented in a sense a Roman fortified equivalent to Offa's Dyke. Tacitus provides a graphic description of Caratacus' last stand, which has sufficient topographical detail to allow us, with some confidence, to place the site at Llanymynech Mountain on the border of Wales and Shropshire. The defeated British leader then took his only remaining option – to seek sanctuary with Cartimandua of the Brigantes. In AD 51 she handed him over to Rome, showing that her own security mattered more to her than a British crusade.

Caratacus' capture did not, however, remove the dangers; in North Wales, and particularly on Anglesey, were located the sacred groves of the Druids, religious centres which fed British tribal nationalism. In AD 59 the governor, Suetonius Paullinus, was moving in to destroy these when he was stopped in his tracks by a rebellion amongst the Iceni and the Trinovantes led by Boudicca, the widow of the client-king, Prasutagus.

The causes of the outbreak were complex because of the involvement of the two tribes. The chief complaints of the Trinovantes related to the consequences of the decision, in AD 49, to move the legionary garrison out of Colchester, and establish on the site a *colonia* (see Chapter 4) for veterans of Legion XIV; land was confiscated for the town and its associated agricultural allotments, local leaders lost money and some were even put to work in constructing the prestigious temple of the Imperial Cult (see Chapter 5), which occupied a prominent position in the town. These Trinovantian leaders had seen the less acceptable face of the *Pax Romana*. An added problem was probably caused by a decision on the part of Roman money-lenders (who in this instance included Nero's principal adviser, Seneca) to call in loans, which had presumably been made to some tribal leaders to encourage and help them in the early stages of Romanisation (see Chapter 4).

The problem of the Iceni was more specific: when Prasutagus died, Nero evidently decided that the special status of the tribe should not continue; consequently, Boudicca and her daughters were deprived of their inheritance and roughly treated at the instigation of the financial *procurator*, Catus Decianus. The resulting revolt was bitter and bloody; according to Tacitus (whose figures may not be totally reliable) 70,000 people were massacred in the attacks on the Romanised towns of Colchester, London and St Albans. In the case of Colchester, a particular assault was made on the temple; the altar to Victory, which stood outside it, was wrecked, and it appears that the head was wrenched from a bronze statue of the emperor, Claudius, and deposited in the river Alde (in Suffolk), probably as an offering to the local deity represented by the river. Excavations in St Albans have revealed clear signs of the burning associated with the attack in AD 59; the buildings of the towns at this stage will have been predominantly timber. Paullinus managed to bring the outbreak under control, though not before Legion IX had received something of a mauling.

There were clearly lessons to be learned. Despite his distinguished record, the governor, who was at fault in concentrating too much of his attention on his military activities in the west, was sacked, while the financial *procurator*, who had fled the province in panic, was replaced. In addition, Nero sent a commissioner to conduct an enquiry, the result of which was evidently to redress the balance between the imperatives of conquest and consolidation. For the next 10 years no unnecessary military activity was undertaken, and the final conquest of North Wales was left until the Flavian period.

In the 60s, the chief difficulty appears to have been the deteriorating situation amongst the Brigantes. This tribe, described by Tacitus as 'the most populous in Britain', appears to have occupied all of northern England from the north Midlands almost up to the Scottish borders. It is, of course, unlikely that such extensive and intractable terrain was governed on a day-to-day basis in a unified manner, and it is clear that Brigantian territory contained a number of 'sub-groups'; we know of the Setantii and Carvetii in the west, and the Tectoverdi, Corionototae and Gabrantovices in the north-east. Besides these, the coastal area of east Yorkshire was occupied by the Parisi, a tribe whose cultural affinities appear to have been closest to the Coritani, Iceni and Trinovantes. The centre of Brigantian power has proved elusive, but was most likely located east of the Pennines, probably in the shape of the extensive *oppidum* of Stanwick, on the eastern entrance to the Stainmore Pass. The importance of the area will have derived from wealth which depended on the exploitation of the good agricultural land of the Vale of York. This also serves to explain why the Romans built a legionary fortress at York in the early 70s and why, in Hadrian's reign, limited self-administration was given to the Brigantes based upon a centre at Aldborough.

As we have seen, the Romans early on secured the northern flank of the new province by a treaty with the Brigantes' 'queen', Cartimandua. Her chief problem lay in controlling factional disputes within the tribal area, the most serious of which were between herself and Venutius, whom Tacitus described as second only to Caratacus as a British war-lord. Although there is no certainty as to the geographical seat of his power, it appears likely that it was in the south and south-west of the tribal territory, where he could seek support from anti-Roman elements in North Wales. It was probably intended that troops based at a Neronian fort at Chester would police such contacts. In an effort to compose the factionalism, Cartimandua had married Venutius. This union proved, however, to be a stormy one which at times broke out into open conflict. On at least two, and possibly more, occasions, units of the Roman army were forced to intervene, probably from bases in the north-west Midlands such as Littlechester, Wroxeter and Whitchurch. These interventions probably did not lead to permanent occupation in the

60s, but consisted rather of 'search-and-destroy' missions in which some troops marched overland, and met up with others who were probably transported by ship from the Dee and put off in estuaries, such as the Mersey, Ribble, Lune and Kent. When their job was done, they will have returned to their bases. The evidence for this consists principally of find-spots of local copies of Claudian *aes*-coins, which are diagnostic of activity at this period; sites will presumably have consisted of campaign-camps rather than forts, such as the fine example which survives at Mastiles Lane on Malham Moor in the western foothills of the Pennines. It is unclear how far north this activity extended, though the recent discovery of early military sites at Cummersdale and Blennerhasset in north-west Cumbria suggests a desire on the Roman side to separate the Carvetii of the coastal lowlands of Solway from the hillspeople to the south of them.

In AD 69, the problems flared up again: Cartimandua having divorced Venutius, was attacked by him. Venutius chose his moment well, as the Roman army was distracted by the pressures of the civil war which both precipitated and followed the death of Nero in AD 68. Nonetheless, the Romans responded as 'required' by their treaty with Cartimandua; the fighting was evidently tough, as is indicated by a reference by the Flavian poet, Papinius Statius, to daring exploits carried out by a son of the governor, Vettius Bolanus. In the end, however, the Roman army could not do more than rescue Cartimandua; as Tacitus put it, 'Venutius won a kingdom, whilst we got a war'.

The time had clearly come for the incorporation of the Brigantes into the province. The glory of this enterprise has traditionally been ascribed to Agricola as a result of his second campaign in AD 78; however, artefactual and structural evidence from excavated sites makes it clear that the conquest of the Brigantes was conceived by the emperor Vespasian (AD 69–79), and entrusted initially to his son-in-law, Quintus Petillius Cerialis (governor, AD 71–4).

It has long been recognised that Cerialis, moving northwards from Lincoln, established a new fortress at York and a line of forts to separate the Parisi from the Brigantes. He defeated Venutius, probably at Stanwick, and crossed the Pennines by way of Stainmore, where the well-preserved campaign-camp at Rey Cross evidently dates from his governorship. It is now clear that he proceeded to establish a new fort (or vexillation-fortress) at Carlisle, where he was joined by Agricola, at that time commander (*legatus*) of Legion XX, to whom Cerialis had entrusted the control of operations in the west. From bases in the north-west Midlands Agricola had come northwards along the Lancashire coastal plain, and followed the Lune and Eden rivers to Carlisle. It seems that, once again, his 'overland troops' were supported by colleagues disembarked from coastal shipping. These campaigns probably played upon natural divisions amongst the Brigantes and introduced sufficient control to permit Cerialis' successor, Julius Frontinus, to return his attention to completing the conquest of Wales, to which Agricola was to put the 'finishing-touch' when he returned to the province as governor late in the campaigning season of AD 77.

Agricola probably had little work still to do amongst the Brigantes since, according to Tacitus, the greater part of the territory had been conquered or fought over during Cerialis' governorship. It seems likely that in AD 78 he moved northwards on two fronts re-establishing himself at Carlisle and constructing a depot at Corbridge (Red House); these were linked by the road, which since medieval times, has been known as the 'Stanegate'. It is likely, too, that Agricola completed the construction of a new legionary fortress at Chester, established road-links between it and York, and opened up a new military road through the foothills of the Pennines from Chester to Carlisle. This road was to remain the chief northward arterial route for the rest of the occupation.

In his third campaign (AD 79), Agricola extended his two north-ward routes to the Forth and the Clyde, establishing a network of forts in southern Scotland, with the pivotal sites at Newstead and Dalswinton. Tacitus, providing one of his rare place-names, informs us that this campaign reached as far north as an estuary called *Taus*, in all probability the river Tay. This was probably reached, for the moment at least, by a single route in the east leading along the Gask Ridge, which effectively separated the good arable land of Fifeshire from the Highlands of the interior.

In AD 79 Vespasian died, and was succeeded by his elder son, Titus (AD 79–81). This seems to have been taken as an opportunity to review objectives; the visible effect in Britain appears to have been that Agricola's fourth and fifth campaigns involved no further forward movement. The fourth was concerned with fortifying the narrow neck of land between the Forth and the Clyde. The Agricolan line has been slow to emerge because of complications in archaeological interpretations caused by the later building of the Antonine Wall. However, it appears that the forts at Camelon, Mollins and Barochan were elements of Agricola's scheme. Tacitus, on two occasions (*Life of Agricola* 23 and 25), appears to suggest disagreement between those (whom he calls 'cowards') who wanted a permanent halt on the Forth–Clyde line, and those who were convinced that Rome's 'mission' urged them further on.

The fifth campaign has been difficult to place because of problems both in understanding Tacitus' account and in the establishment of what he actually wrote. It is, however, generally felt that the 'new tribes' to whom Tacitus refers were located in south-west Scotland. Tacitus also recounts Agricola's dream of taking a single legion across the Irish Sea to conquer Ireland. Although it is not certain whether Agricola could in fact see Ireland – because it is impossible now to be sure of the location of his vantage-point – the matter has recently attracted new interest because of the discovery of Roman material from the Flavian to Hadrianic periods at a promontory-fort at Drumanagh (County Dublin).

The death of Titus in AD 81 brought to power his younger brother, Domitian (AD 81–96), an emperor who won little popularity in senatorial circles. However, his accession coincided with a renewed forward-movement in Scotland. It is clear that Agricola regarded this as the 'go-ahead' for total conquest, although, as we shall see, Domitian may have had more limited objectives.

Agricola's final campaigns took him to the shores of the Moray Firth. In AD 82, two lines of advance were followed – that already established (in AD 79) from the Forth to the Tay, and a new western marked by the construction of 'glen-blocking' line of forts from the Clyde through Drumquhassle, Menteith, Bochastle, Dalginross and Fendoch to a new legionary fortress (for XX *Valeria Victrix*) at Inchtuthil. This makes it tolerably clear that Agricola expected the British legionary garrison to remain at four; the other three legions were based at Chester (II *Adiutrix*, which had in late Neronian times replaced XIV *Gemina Martia Victrix*), York (IX *Hispana*), and Caerleon (II *Augusta*). Agricola's strategy seems broadly to have been based on disrupting the life and economy of the Caledonians; they were harassed by the joint use of troops who marched overland and others who arrived by sea. They were denied access to the good arable land of the east coast, a tactic which, as we have seen, was foreshadowed by the construction of the watchtowers of the Gask Ridge frontier. Rome no doubt also wished to keep the people of Fifeshire separate from the Caledonians and to utilise their grain production. The 'glen-blocking' forts will have made it much harder for pastoralists to move their stock between summer- and winter-pasture. Such tactics were intended to increase disruption and desperation on the part of the Caledonians and force them to fight sooner rather than later.

It should not, however, be thought that Agricola's progress was untroubled; he nearly lost part of Legion IX in a surprise attack, probably at Dalginross, and Tacitus' description of a ferocious battle which took place in the 'very narrows of the gateway' seems to apply well to the peculiar entrances ('double-claviculars'), which are found on campaign-camps of this phase of activity. Further, a speech which Tacitus put into the mouth of Calgacus, Agricola's opponent, appears to indicate just how stretched were Agricola's resources of manpower in what has been taken as a reference to British auxiliaries fighting on the Roman side.

The final campaign brought the battle and a Roman victory at the elusive site named by Tacitus *Mons Graupius*. It would appear from the logic of the campaign-camps that this site should be sought near to the Moray Firth; but although many proposals have been made, such as Knock Hill (Banff), Durno and Bennachie, the location remains uncertain. One ingenious suggestion is that the name itself represents a manuscript-corruption of Latin words meaning 'Hill X'.

The Roman success provided an opportunity for a further review of objectives; Caledonian fighting-power had been destroyed for a generation. Agricola was recalled to Rome, a move regarded by Tacitus as unreasonable and sinister, but hardly so when we remember that his tenure had been twice the length of that considered 'normal' in the Flavian period. This consideration, and the fact that Agricola wanted to capitalise on his victory in a more immediate and dramatic manner than Domitian had in mind, combined to persuade Domitian and his advisers (who probably included his brother-in-law, the former governor, Petillius Cerialis) that the time had come to consider new policy directions; changes of policy reasonably enough required a new governor.

3

The evolution of the frontier

For Tacitus, Agricola's victory at *Mons Graupius* in AD 83 was a triumph for the general's inspirational leadership and the traditional valour of his troops. In the historian's view, therefore, what followed, represented a sell-out: 'Britain was totally conquered, and immediately allowed to slip from our grasp' (*Histories* I: 2). The reality was more complex; as we have seen, policy in Britain had been under scrutiny since the late 70s, and troop-withdrawals in AD 80 had already indicated that the objective of total conquest might have to be compromised.

Nonetheless, it seems that Agricola's immediate successor continued to operate in Scotland, consolidating the victory. At the same time, however, a new policy was taking shape, for it is evident that a series of new large forts (each of seven to eight acres in size) was being constructed along the line of the Stanegate road between Corbridge and Carlisle; the size of these forts, such as Nether Denton, Carvoran, Chesterholm (Vindolanda) and Newbrough, indicates that they were intended for large garrisons, presumably to cope with the influx of troops who needed to be based there if Scotland were evacuated. Indeed, it is possible that the large fort at Cummersdale (south of Carlisle), if it does not relate to initial conquest, was built at this time with a similar purpose in mind. At the same time, it appears likely that the Stanegate was extended eastwards to the coast through Whickham to South Shields, and westwards to an anchorage at Kirkbride. It seems that the westward extension took the form of a *limes* (frontier), similar to that on the Rhine, for there is evidence of a linear palisade, running-ditch and watchtowers along the southern shore of the Solway. These may have been intended to protect the pro-Roman Carvetii from harassment from across the Solway. The developmental sequence is demonstrated by the fact that one of the watchtowers underlies the eight-acre 'Stanegate' fort at Burgh-by-Sands.

This programme of preparation suggests strongly that the evacuation of Scotland was planned in advance. Coin-evidence from Roman forts in Scotland points to AD 87 – the year in which Legion II *Adiutrix* was transferred to the Danube – as the year of execution of the plan. The new fortress at Inchtuthil was systematically dismantled before it was even completed. It is now believed that the *whole* of Scotland was abandoned as a *single* act rather than that there was a two-stage withdrawal with a short-lived frontier between the rivers Forth and Clyde. Of Scottish sites, only Newstead and Dalswinton appear to have been maintained as outliers of the new 'Stanegate – *limes*'.

An extensive programme of consolidation was put in hand south of the new frontier. The thoroughness of this is well illustrated by the complexity of developments in north-west England. A policing network was introduced into the Lake District, an area which had evidently been largely bypassed in the original conquest. Over the next 20 years or so new forts were constructed at Watercrook (Kendal), Ambleside, Hardknott and Ravenglass, with a line further north from Old Penrith, through Troutbeck and Papcastle, to Maryport. Attention was also given to the development of the infrastructure necessary to secure adequate supplies to the army; road- and water-links were enhanced; manufacturing was encouraged in the towns (*vici*) outside forts; 'specialist' industrial sites were established, as at Holt (Clwyd), Heronbridge and Wilderspool (Cheshire), and Wigan and Walton-le-Dale (Lancashire). Such a picture argues strongly against Tacitus' assertion that Agricola's governorship was followed by negative policies and attitudes.

Evidence from aerial reconnaissance has shown that the Stanegate itself underwent development; the large forts were each reduced in size by approximately one half, and intermediate structures, such as fortlets and watchtowers, were introduced. However, the absence of a Roman account of this period makes it hard to reconstruct the context of these developments. It is possible that the demands of Trajan's Dacian and eastern wars led to further troop-withdrawals from Britain between AD 100 and 117, bringing with them a consequent need to re-deploy some of the forces that were left. A 'strength-report' from Vindolanda (dated to c. AD 100), for example, indicates that a considerable part of the garrison had been seconded for duty elsewhere in the area.

The only clue in the literary sources regarding the course of events in Britain at this time is offered by Hadrian's biographer, Spartianus (in the *Scriptores Historiae Augustae*), who writes (*Life of Hadrian* 5: 2) that when Hadrian became emperor (that is, in AD 117) 'the Britons could no longer be held under Roman control'. Details are, however, totally lacking; it is not known for certain where the trouble was located, or who was causing it. Nor do we have details regarding the measures taken to deal with it. However, individual pieces of evidence may offer clues: for example, the fact that Hadrian made Britain the objective of one of his earliest imperial visits (in AD 121) at the very least suggests that the problem was serious. Moreover, the fact that building work on Hadrian's Wall was one of the results, and the posting to Britain of Legion VI *Victrix*, which already had frontier experience on the Rhine, indicate the likely nature of the difficulties. Recently (1997), a fragment of centurion's tombstone has been found at Vindolanda which fixes the date of death as AD 118, during a period of warfare. It should also be noted that Hadrian appears to have involved himself in speeding up the process of Romanisation – the granting to the eastern Brigantes of *civitas*-status with a centre at Aldborough, a new impetus given to a similar development amongst the Cornovii, with their centre at Wroxeter, and drainage projects in the East Anglian Fens, together with (probably) the construction of a 'prestige-town' at Stonea in Cambridgeshire.

As to the location of the difficulties, it appears that Hadrian's famous 'subdued Britannia' coin-issue of AD 119, together with others with clear overtones of victory, points to military victory in the north of the province; the rocks on the Britannia-coin probably point to a mountainous (and thus northern) location. It is further possible that the long-standing problem regarding the reasons for the initial construction of the western end of Hadrian's Wall in turf (rather than stone) might be answered by suggesting that local commanders began the Wall's construction where there was evidence of disturbance and used materials which they would have regarded as 'normal'. It is worth bearing in mind that one of the problems which evidently led to the reoccupation of southern Scotland under

Antoninus Pius appears to have been located in south-west Scotland. Further, recent excavation at the fort of Birdoswald (on Hadrian's Wall) has revealed in the southern guard-chamber of the west gate an area of exceptionally fine stonework, which *may* have been the remains of a victory-trophy.

The commencement of work on Hadrian's Wall probably came after the military victory and on orders from Rome. However, it took on a new priority with Hadrian's visit – a prestige-project with which the emperor, an architect of some distinction, was personally involved. It was started (or perhaps re-started) in the east, as is shown by an inscription from Jarrow, and was built in stone to the point where it crossed the river Irthing, and (presumably) met up with the western turf-built section which had already been started. That the wall, built of stone to a width of 10 feet and a height of (perhaps) 15 feet, was intended as a powerful statement can hardly be doubted. Local tribesmen were clearly meant to be impressed by the skills of engineering and organisation which its construction represented.

It was not, however, originally envisaged as a *new* frontier, but rather an enhancement of that which already existed along the Stanegate road; the difference was that whereas the Stanegate followed the valleys of the rivers Tyne, Irthing and Eden, Hadrian's Wall occupied the northern crests of those valleys, often enhanced in its statement by the difficulty of the terrain on which it was built (as, particularly, on the Great Whin Sill). The installations already in place on the Stanegate were *not* – at first, at least – abandoned as redundant. Essentially, the Wall was in keeping with Hadrian's imperial policy that the age of unlimited expansion was over, and that security would now be guaranteed with effective statements of Roman power and with the development of prosperity and co-operation amongst the subject populations of the provinces.

In its initial plan, the frontier consisted of the Wall itself, running from Newcastle-upon-Tyne to Bowness-on-Solway, equipped with small fortlets (milecastles) at intervals of one mile, and two watch-towers between each pair of milecastles; the watchtowers had elevated platforms suitable for signalling. The milecastles, which were in effect fortified gateways penetrating the Wall, varied in size and were capable of holding from 12 to 24 men whose jobs must have consisted of guarding access through the Wall and patrolling its top. The Wall's facilities indicate that its primary purposes included security, lateral communication, regulation of north–south movement, and (perhaps) ensuring the collection of the appropriate taxes on goods being transported through the Wall. The milecastles and watch-towers were constructed of stone in the 'stone-section' of the Wall, whilst the milecastles (though *not* the watchtowers) were built of turf and timber westwards from the crossing of the river Irthing. The work of construction was entrusted to the Roman army, principally the three legions, whose work is marked by 'progress inscriptions' (centurial stones) and by some differences in building styles. The Wall was provided with a 'V'-shaped military ditch on its northern side.

In *c.* AD 124, for reasons that are not now clear, a change of plan was introduced; the Wall was reduced in width (to six feet) and a series of large garrison-forts was added to the Wall itself. Because the foundation-builders had made more progress than the Wall-builders, there are stretches where the new 'narrow Wall' was constructed on the front (northern) edge of a 'broad foundation', and foundations for structures of the first plan have been recognised beneath structures of the second plan. An integral feature of this second phase of construc-tion was the digging of a continuous lateral ditch on the southern side of the Wall, known as the *vallum*. Its place in the construction-process is made clear by the fact that it deliberately skirts all of the forts with the exception of Carrawburgh, which occupies the mid-way position between Housesteads and Chesters, and which was probably itself an 'afterthought' to shorten what was otherwise a rather long interval between forts.

Unlike the Wall's northern ditch, the *vallum*-ditch was flat-bottomed, about five feet in width and approximately 10 feet deep with steeply sloping sides. North and south of the ditch there was a cleared strip (or berm), which was bounded by continuous running mounds. These show evidence of careful construction, with a core of earth held in place by stacked turves. It is obvious from this that the mounds were as integral to the *vallum* as was the ditch. The purpose of the feature has often been discussed, but remains unclear; it might have been intended as a line to indicate and enclose the military zone, though a more recent idea is that it acted as a covert route of communications, allowing passage for a line of men whose move-ments would thus be unseen from north and south.

Some forts were kept up to the north of the Wall; in the west, Birrens, Netherby and Bewcastle were maintained. Sometimes called 'outpost-forts', these may have been intended as a shield to separate from their neighbours a portion of the Brigantes who had been cut off by the building of the wall – a suggestion strengthened by the discovery at Birrens of a large-scale relief-carving of a Romanised form of the tutelary deity, *Dea Brigantia*, executed as a 'Winged Victory'. The point is illustrative of the disruption caused to local people by the building of the Wall; part of the tribe was left completely adrift from its kith and kin, whilst archaeological evidence has shown that some farmers had had to be displaced to facilitate the building of the frontier. In the east, forts were maintained at Risingham and High Rochester along the line of Dere Street; their purpose was presumably to keep open a line of communication to the tribe of the Votadini, who were both pro-Roman and significant grain-producers.

As part of the modifications of the mid-120s, the Wall was extended eastwards to a terminal fort at Wallsend, whilst in the west a more complex extension was put in place, running from the Wall's terminal fort at Bowness-on-Solway to a little beyond Maryport. In fact, this was conceived in *two* sections – from Bowness-on-Solway to Cardurnock (on the northern side of the estuary called by the Romans *Moricambe*), and from Skinburness (on the southern side of the estuary) to Risehow. The 'western extension' consists of forts, such as Beckfoot and Maryport, fortlets set at intervals of one mile, and two watchtowers between each pair of fortlets. In addition, linear features link these elements; those in the Cardurnock section are enclosed within a cordon provided by parallel ditches, whilst those of the southern sector are backed by running palisades.

The western extension appears to have had three phases of activity – before and after the reoccupation of Scotland, and in the short break between the two phases of construction on the Antonine Wall. It does not appear that *as a whole* the western extension outlasted the second century. Building materials throughout consisted of earth, turf and timber, with the exception of the watchtowers in the third phase, which were built of stone. Further, many of those structures which have seen excavation appear to have been constructed relatively crudely.

As indicated above, there seems no doubt that the extension was not carried far beyond Maryport; it is at this point of the coast that the flat marshes give way to higher cliffs, and thus greater natural protection. The purpose of this work requires examination. It does not seem satisfactory simply to argue that the western terminus of Hadrian's Wall was vulnerable to outflanking. Rather the western extension should be seen in a broader context. The coastal plain of Solway was fertile land (as is shown by the density of rural settlement upon it), which belonged to the pro-Roman Carvetii; the fertility of the land and the stance of its owners will have made them valuable assets in the supplying of the frontier-garrisons. Already in the pre-Hadrianic period they had been given a system of ditches, palisades and watchtowers to protect their economic wealth from marauders from across the Solway. The Hadrianic system will have provided a stronger deterrent against such raiding. Further, a road from Carlisle to the coast at Maryport will have completed the enclosing of the Carvetii, protecting them from jealous neighbours, such as Brigantian hill-farmers. At the same time, the western extension may have acted as a deterrent to those who sought to avoid their tax-liabilities by crossing from Scotland into the province across the Solway.

It is unclear by what time all these structures were in place, but most estimates put it in the later years of Hadrian's reign. It may have been at about the same time that work was initiated to replace the turf sections of Hadrian's Wall in stone. It remains unclear why turf had been used in the first place, and suggestions based upon shortages of building-stone or limestone (for mortar) sound decidedly lame. As suggested above, the true reason may have sprung from circumstances and timing. A turf rampart would be in need of major refurbishment after about 20 years; thus if these installations were replaced as a single act, it may have been done either late in Hadrian's reign, or perhaps after the final evacuation of Scotland in the 160s. Alternatively, it may not have been done as a single act, but piecemeal as necessary. The opportunity was taken to make some modifications; at Birdoswald, for example, the fort had originally been constructed astride the Wall; in the modification, the new stone Wall was pushed a little to the north, so that it formed the fort's northern defences – again perhaps evidence of an evolving process of fort-configuration on the frontier. Birdoswald may also provide evidence of a piecemeal approach taken to modification, for there is some suggestion that the stone fort here may not have been built until some time early in the third century.

At first sight, it is surprising that, after all the effort involved, within five years of Hadrian's death in AD 138, his successor, Antoninus Pius, had taken a decision to set the Wall aside and reoc-cupy southern Scotland as far as a new wall, constructed of turf, between the estuaries of the Forth and the Clyde. Although explana-tions can be adduced, our lack of good source material again leaves us unable to be certain of the reasons for such a major change of policy.

Part of the explanation may lie in Antoninus' own circumstances:

until AD 137, Hadrian (and everyone else) had expected that the succession would pass to Lucius Aelius, whose future role was indicated by the granting to him of the title, *Caesar*. Aelius, however, died before Hadrian, imposing upon the now ailing emperor the need to appoint a new successor. In a competitive field, Hadrian chose the man whom he probably regarded as a 'safe pair of hands'. It is thus understandable, particularly in view of Antoninus' loyalty to the memory of a predecessor who had always been unpopular (even detested) in senatorial circles, that the new emperor should have wished to make his own clear mark on people's minds; as Claudius probably found a century earlier, there was no more decisive way of doing this than by conquest leading to an extension of empire – especially since Antoninus' reputation was of a man of peace.

In view of this, however, it is unlikely that Antoninus would have been tempted into an aggression which was completely unprovoked. Pausanias, in his *Description of Greece* (written later in the second century), talks of Antoninus moving against the Brigantes and depriving them of land because of their attack on the Genounian region. No degree of ingenuity has managed to produce a totally satisfactory explanation of the meaning of this, though in its context it does emphasise the point that this was a war of necessity. The most convincing explanation is that Pausanias was correct in laying blame on the Brigantes, but managed to confuse the circumstances because he also knew of a European tribe of Brigantes (or Briganti) who were neighbours of the Genauni. We have thus lost the precise context, but not the root cause. We have seen that Hadrian's Wall had severed a group of northern Brigantes from the rest of the tribe; it is conceivable that they were causing trouble in southern Scotland, leading in general to instability in the region and (perhaps) in particular causing aggravation to Rome's regional friends, the Votadini. Some support for such a view comes from the fact that, apart from the new Wall, the most obvious area of *new* fortification is to be found in south-west Scotland (in Annandale and Nithsdale). Further, the heavy fortification of the fort at Birrens seems to suggest that it was regarded as lying in hostile territory. In this case, the reoccupation of southern Scotland would appear to have been directed towards securing internal stability in the region rather than as a defence against outside incursion. It remains unclear whether the new wall was initially meant to be of a permanent or temporary nature.

Plans for the invasion were probably underway as early as AD

139–140, when two building-inscriptions record work at Corbridge under the new governor, Quintus Lollius Urbicus. His presence, incidentally, argues against the idea that Antoninus' resumption of a forward policy in Britain was designed purely to appease the now ageing Trajanic generals who were annoyed and frustrated at what they saw as years of inaction under Hadrian; Lollius Urbicus was a Hadrianic protégé. It is likely that Corbridge was used as the principal base for the operation, and that Dere Street was used both directly to reach the Forth estuary and, by means of a north-westerly branch, to make for the Clyde. Operations in Dumfriesshire were probably managed separately from Carlisle/Stanwix.

As with Hadrian's Wall, the developmental sequence for the Antonine Wall suggests considerable complexity. Although, in the event, the Wall itself and most of its installations were built of turf and timber, two forts – Castlecary and Balmuildy – were constructed in stone; indeed, Balmuildy was equipped with stone wings projecting from its northern wall, as if it was expected to make a junction with a *stone* wall. The fact that Balmuildy is the only fort to have produced an inscription of Lollius Urbicus indicates that it at least represents an early part of the construction. It seems likely that two clear phases of construction can be detected. The first plan closely resembled that for Hadrian's Wall in that it used six forts approximately eight miles apart (Carriden, Mumrills, Castlecary, Auchendavy, Balmuildy and Old Kilpatrick). It is likely that it was intended that the intervening spaces would be filled by fortlets at intervals of one mile, similar to those on Hadrian's Wall except that they were to be defended with their own ditches.

The second phase extended the number of forts – by perhaps an extra 12 or 13, which were generally smaller than those of the primary group. Indeed, some were so small (for example, Duntocher at half an acre) that they were garrisoned by detachments of units which had their principal bases elsewhere in the system. With the construction of the extra forts it remains unclear how many fortlets were built. There were, however, some slighter structures attached to the rear of the Wall, which were probably beacon-stances. All the forts, with the exception of Bar Hill, used the Wall as their own northern ramparts and they and the fortlets (unlike the milecastles of Hadrian's Wall) were surrounded on their remaining three sides by double (or triple) ditch-systems.

The Wall itself, which was 37 miles in length, was built of blocks of turf or clay but laid upon a foundation of cobbles, some 14 feet wide, and revetted with stone kerbs, which were pierced at intervals by drainage-channels. Such is the degradation of the structure that it is impossible now to be certain of its height and configuration. It is felt, however, that it sloped inwards on both sides, rising to a height of 10–12 feet, with a patrol-walk on top which was protected by a wattle fence. However, the erosion of the top of the Wall has removed any clear evidence of such superstructures, and no sign survives either of postholes running vertically through the Wall or of duck-boards, which would have been a prerequisite of a patrol-walk.

To the north of the Wall was a V-shaped ditch, which varied in depth between 6 and 12 feet and which was between 25 and 36 feet wide at the top. The earth from the ditch was placed on the northern lip, making an extra mound (*glacis*) which effectively enhanced the depth of the ditch. Outside the ditch, at Rough Castle, there was a further obstacle in the form of an area of closely-set pits (*lilia*); these were each furnished with a sharpened upturned stake, and covered with branches and bracken, providing an effective 'mantrap'.

As was the case with Hadrian's Wall, the Antonine Wall was equipped with outliers; to the north, the Agricolan road was reopened which led through Camelon, to Ardoch, Strageath and Bertha. This re-use of the Gask Ridge suggests once again the desire to protect the agricultural productivity of Fifeshire which will presumably have been used as part of the provisioning of the garrison of the Antonine Wall. Ardoch, in particular, is striking for its well-preserved quintuple ditch-system. The eastern end of the Wall had its terminal fort detached, at Carriden, and was provided with a south-ward link to Newstead and Corbridge through Cramond and Inveresk. Both of these latter sites probably had harbour facilities by which the Wall could be supplied. In the west, the southern bank of the Clyde estuary was overseen by a fort at Bishopton, and two fortlets at Lurg Moor and Outerwards.

There was neither the need nor the manpower to keep Hadrian's Wall in commission at the same time as the Antonine Wall, thus the *vallum*-ditch was filled and its mounds broken through every 45 yards. Its installations were probably left unmanned and some garrisons moved northwards from other forts in Brigantian territory. It is clear too that the fortifications of the Cumberland coast were also evacuated.

At the least, the new frontier allowed for the proper policing of the tribes of southern Scotland, which was probably largely a matter of protecting Rome's friends from those whose attitude remained more robust. If, as is often supposed, the real enemies of Roman Britain were beginning to emerge in northern Scotland, then the new frontier was effectively brought closer to them by about 100 miles. Unfortunately, the evidence of reaction amongst the British to these frontier-changes is far from clear; however, it is widely believed that amongst the Brigantes, at least, these were disturbed times. The evidence of coin-hoards terminating with issues of Antoninus Pius or Marcus Aurelius is introduced to support the idea. However, the strongest sign is generally thought to be Antoninus' issue in AD 154–155 of a coin depicting a dejected (or defeated) Britannia, which presumably alluded to events which must have occurred in or before AD 153. Usually linked with this is the evidence from many forts of the Antonine Wall and the Scottish Lowlands of two phases of occupation in the Antonine period with a short break between them. Although not capable of *precise* dating, this break does not appear quite to coincide with the issue of the 'dejected-Britannia' coin. Thus, the reason for the break does not seem capable of precise interpretation, nor the question of whether the Romans were forced or chose to leave the Wall. It has been suggested that the evacuation was ordered by the governor of the province but was immediately reversed by the emperor himself, whose prestige-project this was. That it was intended as a permanent, or at least long-term, withdrawal seems clear from the decision to re-occupy the installations of Hadrian's Wall and the Cumberland coast. Another interpretation has been to credit Antoninus with the order to withdraw, whilst his successor, Marcus Aurelius (who came to power in AD 161), decided to re-occupy.

It is unlikely that the circumstances will ever be known for certain, although we have sufficient evidence to show that disturbances, at least at local level, continued spasmodically in the frontier-zone for the remainder of the second century. However, the occupation of the Antonine Wall itself seems to have been brought to an end by the mid-160s. The evidence of both coins and pottery makes it unlikely that occupation was maintained, as some have suggested, until the 180s, let alone the beginning of the third century. Rather, it appears likely that it was Calpurnius Agricola (governor, AD 163–166) who managed the final withdrawal from the Antonine Wall and the re-commissioning of Hadrian's Wall, the coastal fortifications, and a number of forts of the hinterland. The reason for the final withdrawal does not appear to indicate that the problems of the north were now solved, but rather that Marcus Aurelius needed extra troops on the Rhine, the Danube and in the eastern theatre of operations; in reality, other frontiers were probably more disturbed than that in Britain – and, in Roman eyes, of more crucial significance.

Disturbances continued; we hear of Roman troops based near Carlisle celebrating the destruction of barbarians on two occasions – probably to be placed in the reigns of Marcus Aurelius and his son and successor, Commodus. We hear, too, of the annihilation of a band of Corionotatae (probably a Brigantian sub-group who lived near Corbridge). Marcus Aurelius is on record as having sent to Britain 5,500 Sarmatian Iazyges to take on garrison-duties in *c.* AD 175; one group of these, as we have seen, was certainly deployed at Ribchester. Commodus' governor, Ulpius Marcellus (AD 181–184), operated in the north, and the emperor assumed the title *Britannicus* in AD 184, presumably to mark the success of these operations. Deeper into the hinterland, an undated tombstone from Ambleside records, with unusual frankness, the death of a Roman soldier at the hands of the enemy *inside his fort*. Further, Dio Cassius records under the year AD 197 that the Caledonians 'had broken their promises', indicating Roman attempts to buy peace in the north.

It appears that, through the later part of the second century, a policy of 'stick-and-carrot' was applied to the problems of the north, and of trying to set one group against another, rather as Tacitus says of Agricola's governorship a century earlier. The Romans probably did not suffer a major defeat during this period, as was once thought, but rather what might be called 'local difficulties'. However, the fact that they evidently could not put an end to these turned them into a serious problem. It is in this light that we should view the decision of Septimius Severus in AD 208 temporarily to transfer the imperial court to York, so that he could take personal charge of the army in Britain in a final attempt to solve the problems of the northern frontier.

As usual, an imperial visit to Britain has prompted much speculation as to its purpose; in view of the fact that Severus was well-established in power, it seems unlikely that he had the same need of high-profile status that may have prompted the military activities of both Claudius and Antoninus Pius, although it is worth bearing in mind that an emperor who had attached so much importance to the support of the army would have needed continually to pay due regard to the army. It has also been suggested that the British expedition may have been prompted by a desire to give his wayward sons, Caracalla and Geta, something positive to occupy them. Further, it is implied by both Herodian and Dio Cassius that worries about loyalty amongst administrators in Britain may have brought Severus to believe that the morale of the army would benefit from such a visit.

The nature of Severus' tactics makes it clear that he saw the real problem as located in the north-east of Scotland. The overland routes in the Lowlands were not reopened; instead, Corbridge was redeveloped, perhaps for legionary use, and the fort at South Shields (on the Tyne-estuary) was reconstructed as an extensive granary, evidently to supply the campaigning army. Also re-activated was the fort at Cramond (on the Forth-estuary) and the site at Carpow (on the Tay) was re-developed as a legionary fortress. The evidence provided by a coin issued in the name of Caracalla suggests that troops were transported up the east coast, presumably to Cramond and Carpow, in order to conduct campaigns that bore a marked similarity to the last two of Agricola – driving up towards the Moray Firth, perhaps to force the Caledonians into a battle which would provide the Romans with an excuse to commit a calculated act of genocide. The removal of the fighting manpower would provide the breathing-space to allow longer-term solutions to be put in place.

The campaigns are marked by surviving traces of very large marching-camps, capable of housing three legions. Their course, however, was marred by the illness and subsequent death of Severus at York in AD 211, and the consequent handing-over of the practicalities of command to Caracalla. The emperor's death gave Caracalla a higher priority – to return to Rome, establish himself in power and remove the threat which he imagined was posed by his younger brother, Geta. It appears that whatever had been achieved militarily was consolidated by 'diplomacy' – that is, the payment of subsidies to northern Scottish tribes. Although this won the disdain of Roman historians, nevertheless it appears that it did succeed in providing nearly a century of peace on the northern frontier. Thus, the conditions which had been desired for so long as a prerequisite for the progress of Romanisation had now – after a century-and-a-half of campaigning and shifts of policy – been effectively realised.

4

Occupation and its infrastructure

Although traditionally Romans prized military glory highly, it was rarely after Augustus' time seen as an end in itself; rather it created the conditions for the Romanisation of a province, and was thus a prelude to the ability of a province to fulfil its role within the empire (see Chapter 1). As we have seen, it is not always possible in any case to recover the anatomy of conquest itself because so many of the temporary campaign-camps which will have marked its course have succumbed to the ravages of time. Maps of Roman Britain essentially present us with the anatomy of *occupation and administration*; although much of northern Britain remained within a military occupation, the Lowland zone of the south largely passed out of direct military oversight.

The administration of Britain was carried out by a relatively small number of Roman officials, whilst much day-to-day work was entrusted to Romanised British, whose chief qualifications for the task were their loyalty and wealth. Although the structure of occupation changed over the years, at first, Britain was administered as a single province (*Britannia*), with both military and civilian authority residing in the governor (*Legatus Augusti Pro Praetore in Britannia*). The administrative centre of the province was initially sited at Colchester but soon transferred to London.

In the first two centuries AD, the governor, a senior senator, held responsibility for both the conquest and the military occupation; he also controlled a range of administrative and judicial activities, which included oversight of the tribal *civitates* and the trial of cases involving those who were not Roman citizens. Apart from his 1,000-strong bodyguard (*singulares consulares*), he had a relatively small staff of administrative and clerical assistants and soldiers undertaking policing duties. The range of duties clearly represented a heavy burden, to which we should add frequent and detailed correspondence with the emperor, the nature of which we can judge by that which passed between Pliny and Trajan, when the former was governor of Bithynia (*Letters*, Book X). It appears that, at times at least, perhaps when the workload was particularly heavy, the governor received assistance from a legal expert, the *legatus iuridicus*. It has been suggested that this may have happened at times when questions of landownership arose, as when the *civitates* were being established.

The major area which lay outside the governor's competence was that concerned with financial and economic affairs, including taxation and the administration of a range of imperial estates (concerned principally with agriculture and mining). Such matters were handled by an officer of equestrian status, the *Procurator Augusti*, who had under him a staff of junior *procuratores* concerned with particular regions or undertakings. The chief *procurator* was an imperial appointment responsible directly to the emperor for a province's budget. Because of the nature of the job, it could on occasion enjoy a very high profile, as when, in Nero's reign, Catus Decianus had to handle the transfer of Prasutagus' kingdom to the provincial administration – in that case, with disastrous consequences. It is possible that as a result of this experience there was some adjustment of 'job-descriptions' as, according to Tacitus, Agricola 'interfered' in taxation-matters to check abuses. The logic of this would have stemmed from the governor's responsibility for local government (*civitates*); local leaders would clearly have had greater difficulty in meeting their financial obligations if they were losing money to corrupt tax-collectors.

The *procurator* was responsible for the collection of taxes of all kinds; this will have included the tax on grain and other agricultural produce, such as hides (for tents), and the taxes that were raised on the movement of goods into and out of the province; the trade that is evident with Scotland will have guaranteed considerable tax-revenue which was collected on Hadrian's Wall. In addition, the *procurator* was responsible for the management of all imperial estates; some of these will have been concerned with agricultural produce, and we hear, for example, of a *procurator* for weaving at Winchester. He will also have decided the manner of exploitation of all mineral resources; in particular decisions had to be made as to whether a resource would be exploited directly, as at the gold mines at Dolaucothi in Carmarthenshire, where the activities were overseen by soldiers in the nearby fort at Pumsaint. Alternatively, he might work out leasing-agreements which will have fixed with private companies the volume of the resource required by the government and together the sizes of workforces and the number of days to be worked which effectively determined profit-levels. Ingots offer clues as to the manner of exploitation; from North Wales we have lead ingots which evidently resulted from centralised extraction, whilst some from the Peak District bear the marks of private companies. A highly important aspect of the *procurator's* job was the earmarking of land to be used for the settlement of military veterans; this in its turn will have had a major impact on the overall pattern of landownership and agricultural exploitation.

In terms of seniority, those closest to the governor were the legionary commanders (*legati legionis*), who were senators of praetorian standing. They could deputise for the governor when necessary and, as Tacitus shows, could share with him the onus of command during campaigns. Apart from those senators who might be in a province on their own business, and who could in those circumstances be used by the governor as temporary advisers, the only other officials of high rank (though too young formally to have acquired senatorial status) were the military tribunes in the legions (*tribuni militum*). According to Tacitus, however, these men, who were meant to be serving a military apprenticeship, more often than not used their appointments to enjoy themselves.

This relatively small establishment, then, was responsible for all tasks in the province relating to security and administration – either directly through their own staffs or through local personnel to whom the work might be delegated. Since the time of Augustus, when a decision had been made regarding the supportable size of the Roman army, it had been impossible to govern provinces without an input of local wealth and talent. In Britain, the undertaking of the work of local government by the wealthy, many of whom were probably descended from the old tribal hierarchies, was a crucial part of the overall pattern of administration. Such men, by background and status, shared the oligarchic aspirations of Romans themselves and so developed an effective rapport with the occupiers.

By and large, in Britain the pre-Roman tribal system was adapted to form the building-blocks of the local administration, so that the *civitates* broadly respected the pre-Roman political geography, but also took account of current needs. At first, however, the province will have been directly under the governor's supervision with the exception of those areas which were, presumably under arrangements made by Claudius himself, left in the hands of local grandees. This happened in at least part of the Atrebatic kingdom – presumably the part later referred to as the *civitas* of the Regnenses ('the people of the kingdom') – and in the territory of the Iceni; Cogidubnus and Prasutagus respectively acted as 'client-monarchs' for the conquerors. An inscription from Chichester refers to 'Tiberius Claudius Cogidubnus, king and *legatus* of the emperor in Britain'; the form of his name indicates that Cogidubnus had been granted full Roman citizenship by Claudius.

It is not clear at what stage or at what pace the formation of self-administering *civitates* was undertaken; Tacitus' language indicates that Agricola had a major hand in it, and an inscription from St Albans appears to confirm this. It is probably safer to see it as an aim, rather than as a definite process, occurring as and when an area appeared ready to take on the responsibilities. It is possible that some moves were made in the wake of Boudicca's revolt, though earlier references to loans made by Nero's adviser, Seneca, suggests that this did not mark the beginning of the process, since the most obvious purpose of such loans would have been to finance the establishment of a *civitas*. The northward movement of the army in the Flavian period meant that many areas in the southern half of the province were released from direct military occupation and will have required a civilian alternative. Even so, although practical help in building was available from legionary sources, the pace of change in individual areas will have been determined by the level of wealth of local leaders; in the case of the *civitas* of the Cornovii, for example, the process probably started when, in the later 70s, Wroxeter was abandoned as a legionary base in favour of Chester. However, an inscription from Wroxeter suggests that the *civitas* was not up and running until Hadrianic times and it appears likely that the Cornovii had found it difficult to acquire the funds that they required.

It is clear that, after the experience of Boudicca's rebellion, care will have been required over the advancement of the Iceni, who may not have reached *civitas*-status until the Trajanic period. It was Hadrian who, probably on his visit to Britain in AD 121–122, inaugurated the *civitas* of the Brigantes by releasing eastern parts of the former kingdom into the hands of local administrators. Further, the

41

process continued as appropriate; for example, the Carvetii, a sub-group of the Brigantes in northern Cumbria, evidently reached *civitas*-status in the third century AD. As we have noted, the physical boundaries of the *civitates* did not necessarily respect pre-Roman territorial divisions – if, of course, these were clear, anyway; thus, the territory of the Atrebates was divided between three *civitas* authorities – the Atrebates (at Silchester), the Regnenses (at Chichester), and the Belgae (at Winchester). Further, it appears that later on the *civitas* of the Durotriges was subdivided to give a new *civitas*, with its centre at Ilchester.

The process, which is often referred to as the urbanisation of Roman Britain, was in fact less to do with the building of towns as an objective in itself than with the establishment of the *civitates*, or administrative areas. In Roman eyes, towns simply constituted natural administrative centres in such areas. Prior to Caracalla's decree of universal Roman citizenship to the free-born (the *constitutio Antoniniana* of AD 212), towns formed a significant hierarchy in the Roman empire. At the top, there were the *coloniae*, which, following a long Roman tradition going back to the fourth century BC, were 'plantations' of Roman citizens, often in freshly won territory. In return for the privilege of a certain degree of local autonomy, in which they elected their own officials and local senate, the colonists accepted the obligation of forming a military reserve and taking on responsibility for Romanising surrounding territory (*territorium*). Because local marriage was envisaged for colonists such towns appeared, after a time, to be little different in terms of population from other types, though pride in their origins and traditions probably gave the inhabitants a feeling of superiority over other towns: it is known, for example, that in Gaul the inhabitants of the *colonia* at Lugdunum (Lyons) entertained considerable contempt for those of neighbouring Vienna (Vienne).

In the first century AD, *coloniae* were established at Colchester (AD 49), Lincoln (AD 92), and Gloucester (AD 97). The extra-mural settlement outside the fortress at York received a grant of *colonia* status early in the third century. Legally, the land which was assigned to a *colonia* did not form part of the *territorium* of the relevant *civitas*, though in some cases – for example, Colchester – the *colonia* seems to have acted as a *de facto civitas*-centre, 'robbing' nearby Chelmsford of much of its potential significance. In the case of Gloucester, however, the neighbouring *civitas*-centre at Cirencester always seems to have been economically more vibrant. It is possible, too, that the evident lack of success at the *civitas*-centre of the Parisi at Brough-on-Humber was caused by its proximity to York. In the *coloniae*, the local officials ('magistrates') and senate provided an administration closely modelled upon that of the old Roman republic; whilst they were not, of course, outside the governor's jurisdiction, as Roman citizens they possessed what others in the province did not, the liberty of an ultimate 'appeal to Caesar'.

Second in the urban hierarchy were the *municipia*, towns of local origin whose citizens had been granted either complete or half Roman citizenship. The inhabitants organised their affairs rather as did those in the *coloniae* and, it is assumed, doubled with a local administrative role. The identities of *municipia* in Roman Britain are not altogether clear. St Albans appears to have enjoyed the status, though it is not clear precisely when it was awarded; Tacitus seems to suggest that it was a *municipium* at the time of Boudicca's rebellion, though some believe that the status was not granted until Flavian times. The clue to the identification of St Albans as a *municipium* is the appearance of its name without an attached indication of *civitas*; on such a criterion, it is believed that London enjoyed the status, and (by some) that Leicester did also.

The majority of the administrative towns, however, were those known as *civitas*-centres. In terms of appearance and, indeed, in some areas of administration they were little different from *coloniae* and *municipia*, but the members of the *civitates* were not Roman citizens and were thus totally subject to the jurisdiction of the governor, including his right of summary jurisdiction (*ius gladii*). The chief qualification for the job of leadership in the *civitates* was wealth, which may have come through commerce but which was more likely to have derived from land-ownership. Many such local leaders were descendants of the old pre-Roman tribal aristocracies, as is sometimes betrayed in their names – such as Lucullus, son of Amminius, whose name is found inscribed on an altar from Chichester. These men were responsible both to the provincial governor and to the *procurator* for different aspects of their jobs, which included responsibility for the establishment and upkeep of buildings and services and for good order in their *civitates*; they were also responsible for the collection of and, where appropriate, making good shortfalls in the taxes due from members of their communities. It is little wonder that as the administrative costs and burdens of local government increased, particularly from the later third century, it became more difficult to find a large supply of men willing and able to carry out such functions. Because of this, local office may have been made hereditary.

Of course, not all of the province's inhabitants were members of *civitates*; some areas remained under a direct military jurisdiction. This appears to have been the case in the frontier-zone and in much of north-west England. Here, the administrative centres were the individual Roman forts, with the fort-commanders (usually men of equestrian status) taking responsibility for all decision-making involving both military and civilian personnel in their *territoria*. Although the precise extent of each fort-*territorium* cannot now be reconstructed, we can assume that, in the security-network constituted by the distribution of forts, all areas will have owed responsibility to a fort-commander, and that all civilians, whether farmers or inhabitants of the small towns which grew outside Roman forts (*vici*), will have come under his jurisdiction.

These officials were the source of permission for all non-military buildings, and could, it seems, require the removal of any that conflicted with military imperatives: it is certain, for example, that local farmers were ordered to quit if their farms happened to be situated on land required for military purposes, such as the farm which lay between Hadrian's Wall and the *vallum* at Milking Gap in Northumberland. It is, in fact, found with increasing frequency that Roman forts were constructed not on land that first had to be cleared of woodland, but which had already been under the plough.

In the cases of farmers within his *territorium*, the fort-commander will have decided on the matter of contracts between his fort and local producers – as is indicated by the writing-tablets from Vindolanda (Northumberland) – and this presumably included the nature of produce to be supplied and, in the case of animals required for food, such matters as the optimum age for slaughter. In the small towns outside the forts there was evidently no right of local self-administration, though 'unofficial' groups probably existed such as the assembly (*curia*) of the Tectoverdi; it is also likely that civilians could meet on religious business, as is indicated by an altar to the smith-god, Vulcan, from Vindolanda, which was erected by a group describing themselves as 'the townspeople of Vindolanda' (*Vicani Vindolandenses*). As we shall see, life in such towns was probably in practice vibrant both socially and economically but, without such status-promotions as evidently happened at Carlisle when the *civitas* of the Carvetii was established, ultimately lacking in the opportunity for political and administrative development.

Whilst the administrative infrastructure probably continued to develop along the lines sketched above at least into the fourth century, the governing superstructure underwent significant changes. The first came in the time of Septimius Severus (AD 193–211), when the single province was divided into two – *Britannia Superior* in the south with its centre at London, and *Britannia Inferior* in the north with its centre at York, where the governor also had command of Legion VI *Victrix*.

The second was the work of Diocletian (AD 284–306) who, aware of the anarchic chaos which characterised much of the third century, introduced a wholesale reform of imperial administration, the chief purpose of which was to fragment the command-structure to the point where no single official was likely to be able to amass the resources necessary to mount a credible challenge to Diocletian himself. Four provinces were now created in Britain: *Britannia Prima* with its centre at Cirencester; *Britannia Secunda* with its centre at York; *Flavia Caesariensis* with its centre at Lincoln; and *Maxima Caesariensis* of which London was the centre. It has been suggested by some that a fifth province, *Valentia*, was added later in the fourth century. However, it seems altogether a more plausible suggestion that *Valentia* was an honorific title, deriving from the name of the then-emperor (Valentinian I) and applied to the whole of Britain, following its recovery from the effects of the 'barbarian conspiracy' of AD 367.

The administration which was put in place was very bureaucratic. The top level, the division of the empire into four parts (in AD 293), put Britain into the portion attributed to the western junior emperor (*Caesar*), Constantius Chlorus. The British provinces were administered for him by a *vicarius* based at London, who was himself responsible to an intermediate tier of administration, in the shape of the praetorian prefect for the Gauls. Responsible to the *vicarius* were the four civilian provincial governors (entitled either *praesides* or *consulares*), whose authority embraced much of what had originally fallen to the governor in his civilian capacity, and the financial *procurator*. Diocletian's reforms took military authority out of the governor's hands by creating two new commanders – *Dux Britanniarum* ('Duke of the Britains') and *Comes Litoris Saxonici* ('Count of the Saxon Shore') – which were responsible for frontier-armies. In emergencies, elements of a mobile field army, responsible directly to a tetrarch, could be sent into Britain under a chosen commander. This burdensome bureaucracy will obviously have added considerably to the financial obligations set upon wealthy provincials, who had to undertake the administrative tasks outlined in this chapter.

Such changes in administration, however, point clearly to two important considerations: first, they indicate the continuing importance which was attached to Britain's place in the Roman empire; second, they demonstrate the ability of the provinces to create sufficient wealth to cope with the burdens. Finally, it should be noted that the willingness of local people to undertake the burdens without too much complaint points to the overall success in the process of turning the British into 'Romano-British'.

5

Economy and society in Roman Britain

The barbarians were adapting themselves to Roman ways, were becoming accustomed to hold markets, and were meeting in peaceful assemblages. They had not, however, forgotten their ancestral habits, their native manners, their old life of independence, or the power derived from arms. Hence, so long as they were unlearning these customs gradually and by the way, as one may say, under careful watching, they were not disturbed by the change in their manner of life, and were becoming different without knowing it.

So wrote the third-century historian, Dio Cassius (56.18: 2–3), of the progress of Romanisation along the Rhine at the time of the Varus disaster of AD 9. Tacitus, albeit more cynically, makes similar points with regard to the British during the first century AD:

They [the Britons] have not yet been softened by protracted peace. The Gauls, too, we have been told, had their hour of military glory; but then came decadence with peace, and valour went the way of lost liberty. The same fate has befallen such of the Britons as have long been conquered; the rest are still what the Gauls used to be.

(*Life of Agricola* 11)

and:

> The following winter [AD 78–79] was spent on schemes of the most salutary kind. To induce a people, hitherto scattered, uncivilised and therefore prone to fight, to grow pleasurably inured to peace and ease, Agricola gave private encouragement and official assistance to the building of temples, public squares and private mansions. He praised the keen and scolded the slack, and competition to gain honour from him was as effective as compulsion. Furthermore, he trained the sons of the chiefs in the liberal arts and expressed a preference for British natural ability over the trained skill of the Gauls. The result was that in place of distaste for the Latin language came a passion to command it. In the same way, our national dress came into favour and the toga was everywhere to be seen. And so the Britons were gradually led on to the amenities that make vice agreeable – arcades, baths and sumptuous banquets. They spoke of such novelties as 'civilisation', when really they were only a feature of enslavement.
>
> (*Life of Agricola* 21)

As we have seen (Chapter 1), an aim of conquest and occupation was to create provinces that were economical to run peacefully; the passages of Dio Cassius and Tacitus provide an indication of what was desired, whilst Tacitus' description of Agricola's contribution provides some information on methods employed to achieve this. The necessary prerequisites to a successful process of involving local people in their own administration were the appropriate attitude of mind, the existence of incentives and a culture of wealth-creation. In this way, the Roman occupation would be able to utilise the services of the local upper classes who would certainly not have agreed with the observation put by Tacitus into the mouth of the Caledonian chieftain, Calgacus: 'They create a desolation, and call it peace.'

It is clear from Tacitus' description of the British environment (*Life of Agricola* 12) that it was regarded as generally favourable for the development of a society whose essential preoccupations were materialistic. It is worth bearing in mind that, on the evidence of Strabo, the south of the country had been producing an exportable surplus of grain even before the conquest and that, on the evidence of archaeology, a strong trade had already developed between some British tribes and the Mediterranean world. The Roman occupation offered the means for the continued prosperity of a wealth-based aristocracy which, in its turn, provided a supply of the type of people with whom the Romans preferred to deal.

As Tacitus shows, Agricola's technique was to combine a conciliatory attitude with encouragement, inducement and education; there are, in fact, two inscriptions from York in Agricola's time which mention the presence there of a known teacher, Demetrius of Tarsus. Organisation, communications, and a large and well-paid market for local goods in the shape of the army were factors which transformed the encouragement into real progress towards Romanisation. Ultimately the inducements to the British tribal aristocracies and their descendants to co-operate with Rome were the opportunities to enhance their wealth and to maintain power and local patronage, albeit within well-prescribed limits.

There is no doubt that, although it is appropriate to use the term 'Romanisation' of the whole of the province (see later), it is more obvious in a physical form in the Lowland zone of the south, where Romanised towns and villa-estates were more densely distributed. In the west, this pattern extended approximately to the borders of Shropshire and Cheshire, whilst in the east it can be traced up as far as north Yorkshire and County Durham. Romanisation of a different physical appearance characterised remaining parts of the north and north-west.

Yet the impetus towards all of the Romanisation lay originally in military occupation; many of the southern forts were probably not evacuated until the renewal of the military advance northwards in the 70s. Thus, an important element of developing wealth for local people will have been the market constituted by these troops. This will have encouraged the growth of towns outside the forts; such towns may, as the military moved on, have developed into the types described in Chapter 4.

Obviously Romanised towns will, in many ways, have represented a cultural change from what had happened before the Roman occupation had begun. But the change must not be exaggerated. Many of the British had lived in, or at least during troubled times retreated temporarily to, hillforts. From the Roman point of view these were inaccessible, since they lay off the routes of communication and were inconvenient for such services as running water. Yet those that had seen permanent habitation will have been organised themselves in functional terms – perhaps with areas set aside for religious and industrial purposes, and providing for services such as education, trade and entertainment. In so far as Romanised towns will also have provided for such functions and services, the change experienced by the British will therefore have proved less dramatic than might be assumed.

As in the north later, a town outside a fort (*vicus*) will usually have been a vibrant concern, but will have lacked public buildings and often have appeared 'ramshackle'. It will probably have had no nucleus and no plan of development, but instead will have grown spontaneously, tailing off into a kind of rural suburbia. If such a town was to develop, after a military evacuation, along Romanised lines, then re-planning will have been required. In some cases, particularly in the south-east, where a different kind of pre-Roman centre existed on Lowland territory, the Roman fort/fortress and town could develop over it and therefore as a direct continuation of it. Thus, at the time of conquest, a fortress was established on a portion of Cunobelinus' centre (*oppidum*) at Colchester and, six years later, following military evacuation, was modified and extended into the *colonia*.

It is evident at Colchester and elsewhere that the 'independent' town could utilise the military street-system, modifying it to an urban shape. This process entailed using the old alignments to create blocks of space (*insulae*) in which the various public and private buildings could be located. Thus, the whole town would have assumed 'a well-built appearance'. At the centre of such a town was a square (or *forum*) which served as both an administrative and commercial centre, where on market-days the permanent shops would have been joined by temporary stalls as traders came into town to buy and sell. It is again evidence of such 'encouragement and assistance' as Tacitus ascribes to Agricola that the basic format of the Romano-British *forum* represented a version, ameliorated for the urban context, of the military headquarters (*principia*). It seems likely that, although the British had to finance such ventures, the blueprints and skilled manpower derived from legionary sources. A similar military 'influence' can be seen in the 'linear' arrangement of public bath houses and the resemblance between an essentially simple style employed for civilian theatres and amphitheatres and military versions of the latter (as are still to be seen outside the fortresses at Caerleon and Chester).

Few major Romano-British towns have seen extensive excavation; indeed, it is a comment on the success of most of these foundations that they have survived as major towns or cities to the present day, thus denying physical access to a great deal of information regarding their earlier phases. Excavation at Silchester, however, has revealed a town with a range of public and private buildings, temples and industrial facilities such as dyeing-works and tanneries which indicate a close integration between the town and its rural hinterland. Such facilities argue strongly against the view, once commonly accepted, that the towns of Roman Britain were 'parasitic' in their relationship with the countryside. At Silchester and elsewhere, houses in a range of styles have been found. There was evidently no shortage of people living in towns, even if their 'main residences' may have been in the country. It is doubtful whether residence-patterns can be used as the sole criterion of the success or failure of a town, particularly when it was a common feature of Roman aristocratic practices, which were being emulated, to share one's residence time between town and country. Nor can we, in assessing a town's possible success, rely on the criterion of empty space or 'black earth', as there is no reason why those who lived in Romano-British towns should not also have had land for horticultural purposes within the town-area.

In any case, we have sufficient evidence to suggest that if a town was a failure in the sense of having no obvious and unique role to play in its own area, it would wither. We have already seen that Chelmsford and Brough-on-Humber, although having an administrative role within their *civitates*, 'lost out' commercially to Colchester and York respectively. Similarly, a later (Hadrianic) urban foundation at Stonea in Cambridgeshire evidently failed because it could not create a distinctive role for itself in an already established local economy. By contrast we can cite the case of Cirencester, which evidently proved to be an ideal replacement for the nearby British site at Bagendon. Commercially, Cirencester was sufficiently successful to attain a 'specialised' market-building (*macellum*) in addition to the facilities available in its *forum*. Not only this, but it also found a major business in providing mosaic-floors for villas in its hinterland. The token of its success is ultimately the fact that it was chosen as one of the 'capital cities' of the four Diocletianic provinces of Britain. In contrast to Chelmsford, the commercial vibrancy of Cirencester clearly outstripped the neighbouring *colonia* at Gloucester.

Thus, towns which were given, or which carved out for themselves, sustainable roles would succeed; the degree of that success obviously depended upon whether its role was unique in its area and indeed how large was the area which looked to it as the centre of its commercial, cultural and administrative life. As we have seen, many of the towns of the Lowland zone, which developed to success started as 'service-towns' (*vici*) outside forts. In the north of the province, where *civitates* were not established at first, these *vici* remained and their remains help not only to enlighten us about their own development, but also to offer a natural comparison with the towns of the south, together with clues to the early development of these.

As we have seen, the most obvious difference between the *vici* and the *civitas*-centres was the absence in the former of an administrative role. They were governed by the commanders of the adjacent forts. The principal role of the *vici* was to 'service' the needs of those in the fort and, of course, their own inhabitants. Roman soldiers were well-paid, and could, therefore, afford the goods and services which were the 'products' of the *vici*. These would obviously include a wide range of manufactured items – pots, tools, jewellery, religious objects, clothes, shoes – as well as drink and food, which might well be purchased in cooked form from a 'take-away outlet'. Those providing services of varying kinds included sculptors, doctors, and owners of bars, gambling-houses and brothels. A large proportion of the population, however, comprised the unofficial wives and families of serving soldiers – unofficial, because whilst the law (prior to the reign of Septimius Severus) prevented legalised marriages for soldiers, little notice was taken of relationships that existed. Indeed, the discharge-certificates (diplomas) of Roman soldiers retrospectively provided legitimacy for the children of such, unofficial liaisons. Thus, upon discharge, many soldiers simply 'retired' to live in the adjacent *vicus*, perhaps with a business already established.

An important element of the 'services' provided by a *vicus* to both soldiers and civilians lay in the field of religion. Some religious observances, of course, centred upon the fort itself – the 'imperial cult', state-deities such as Jupiter, Mars and Hercules, and other gods who may have had an especial significance for the unit in garrison. Other cults, however, had their centres in the *vici*; many of these (see chapter 6), because of the constant diversification and movement of commercially-based populations, were probably transitory in their observance. Others, such as the smith-god, Vulcan, had a more permanent place because of the permanence of the trades over which they presided. It is not uncommon, presumably because of considerable numbers of local people present in *vicus*-populations, for Celtic deities, albeit in a Romanised form, to appear without the usual 'twinning' with a Roman equivalent. Thus, we find a shrine to Antenociticus at Benwell and Cocidius at Bewcastle (both in the frontier-zone).

It is evident from the writing-tablets found at Vindolanda that the fort and *vicus* developed a commercial relationship with the farmers of their hinterlands. Grain was brought into the *vicus* (either requisitioned or commercially) for processing into food and drink. We learn from one tablet that a single *denarius* (a day's pay for a legionary soldier) would purchase 800 boot-nails, 32 eggs, seven and a half pounds of bacon or 144 pints of beer! This, apart from providing a valuable insight into the purchasing-power of military pay, offers an insight into items of agricultural origin which might find their way to the shops of *vicus*-traders. Such insights, of course, serve to provide an idea of the scale of the agriculture in the hinterland of a Roman fort, and thus the scale of woodland-clearance, which in many cases seems significantly to pre-date the establishment of fort and *vicus*. It is unlikely, however, that military *vici* would have been able easily to support an independent existence for long; as established, their hinterlands were relatively small, and the presence of their military market was vital. This is demonstrated by the fact that when in the third century, the *civitas* of the Carvetii was established in the frontier-zone, the hinterland of Carlisle at its centre probably extended across the Solway Plain and along the valley of the river Eden, and perhaps some of the way down the Lune valley, thus 'swallowing' the hinterlands of a number of existing *vici*.

As we have seen, all types of town supported a range of industries, in some cases (as at the *vicus* at Manchester) concentrated into 'industrial estates'. The provision of the raw materials of these industries suggests the substantial development of relevant sources. Many of those involved in industry will clearly have made a living from helping to supply a largely local market, although the Roman army required a range of products in greater bulk than could be produced locally.

At first, the evidence suggests that individual units of the army set up their own facilities for manufacturing pottery and a range of building-materials. Some of these, such as Holt and Heronbridge, servicing the legionary fortress at Chester, operated on a local basis throughout the second century. However, from the later first century the army was beginning to think in more global terms, placing large contracts in the hands of area-wide (or even province-wide) manufacturers. Tableware of good quality (such as Samian pottery) was imported into Britain in bulk, but probably distributed to town-shops by itinerant traders; the same was probably true for British fine-ware, such as that manufactured in potteries in the Nene Valley.

However, the ubiquitous 'black-burnished' ware, a type of cooking-pot found in large quantities on all military sites, was probably ordered by the army on a bulk-contract placed with manufacturers in southern England. A similar arrangement with the Crambeck potters of Yorkshire seems to have facilitated the supply of such vessels in the later fourth century.

There was also scope, however, for the establishment of 'regional facilities'; a good example of such an arrangement is provided by the complex site at Wilderspool (on the river Mersey, south of Warrington). Here, a wide variety of industrial processes was carried out on a site housing mostly local workers. Their products have been traced as far away as the Antonine Wall. The army probably bought in bulk from such a complex, and put the material into depot-storage until it was required, at sites such as Walton-le-Dale (on the river Ribble) and Corbridge.

A large number of people were undoubtedly involved in the range of manufacturing and processing industries mentioned above, as well as in the extraction of necessary raw materials and the transporting of these and the finished products. Most will have come from various parts of Britain, but some originated from distant parts of the empire, such as Barates, the sculptor, who worked at South Shields, but who came from Palmyra in Syria. Most of the doctors whose names appear in inscriptions came from the eastern Mediterranean, whilst the personnel of the Roman army, although of course Romanised, had their origins in a wide variety of mostly European provinces. Britain's working population must, therefore, have been cosmopolitan, and it will thus have been a cosmopolitan, but Romanised, world into which the British were drawn. All, however, contributed to a culture which developed as distinctively Romano-British.

The bulk of the working population, however, was engaged in agriculture on a variety of scales. This, too, will have presented a cosmopolitan appearance, although it is no longer believed that the legions were followed by large numbers of people seeking to exploit the land. The process of demobilisation from the army over time ensured that the origins of those working the land in Britain were diverse.

The chief contrast in the rural landscape between the Lowland and Highland zones lay in the density of villa-estates in the former. North of the Humber estuary villas become far less frequent, whilst in the west, beyond the north Midlands, they are virtually non-existent. We should not, however, be tempted to draw too radical conclusions from this about the progress of Romanisation. Nor should we assume that rural development in the south conformed to a particularly simple pattern. Villas existed in different styles and degrees of complexity, and were not the only type of rural buildings. Alongside them were much more simple sub-rectangular and sub-circular structures whose obvious structural affinities lay in the north of the province.

Most villas were not simply country-residences but the nerve-centres of agricultural estates. Although individual ownership would be hard to prove, it is likely that many of these were owned either by the descendants of the tribal aristocracies or by soldiers discharged from the Roman army. Whilst it is evident that considerably more land had been cleared of forests before the Roman conquest, the occupiers' need of wood for building and fuel continued the process, clearing more land for cultivation. Some regeneration of woodland was however necessary to match continuing demand.

It was long assumed that villa-estates followed an established pattern of development – from small 'cottages' in the first century, the 'winged-corridor' type in the second, as at Ditchley (Oxfordshire), and finally (in some cases) to a full courtyard type in the later third and fourth centuries, such as Bignor (West Sussex), Brading (Isle of Wight), or Chedworth (Gloucestershire). Although all three types of villa are found, the assumed chronology and pattern of development now seem far too inflexible. It seems clear that villa-development matched the resources of the villa-owners. Whilst most sites which developed from Iron-Age farms in the first century AD assumed the style of the box-like 'cottage-farm', other more lavish structures can be found in the first century – for example, Fishbourne (Sussex), Rivenhall (Essex) and Eccles (Suffolk). Further, 'cottage-farms' appear for the first time late in the Roman period, representing the point when the owner could afford to improve his farm. The fact that some sites show the 'assumed' pattern of development is a reflection of developing success and prosperity amongst some villa-owners. Nor should we assume that everyone, even in the south, could afford, or chose, to follow a Romanised form of development. Some farms of the 'Iron-Age' type continued throughout, and we should not assume that their owners necessarily remained marginal or hostile to the process of Romanisation. More likely, their resources remained more limited than those of others.

The complexity of a rural site might reflect the desire of a wealthy owner to make an ostentatious display of that wealth with buildings devoted to luxurious living. Such sites would often boast refinements such as private bath-suites, mosaic floors and painted wall-decorations. In many cases, however, structural complexity might have come about because of a diversification of wealth-generating activities. Agricultural products were 'processed' on the spot on some farms, although the majority of farmers probably took advantage of facilities available in nearby towns. Thus cattle and sheep might be taken to town 'on the hoof' for butchering. Recent evidence from Stonea (Cambridgeshire), for example, has shown that meat-preservation was conducted there in bulk, perhaps in fulfilment of official contracts to supply the army. Many towns had businesses devoted to tanning and weaving, indicating that town-facilities were indispensable to the generation of rural wealth and further undermining the long-held view that the towns of Roman Britain were 'parasitic'.

It is often argued that the north of the province did not share in either the prosperity or the Romanisation of the south. It is true that the rural landscape of the north presented a very different *physical* appearance from that of the south. Few villas were found, but rather sub-rectangular and sub-circular huts – either singly or in much more complex developments, as at Ewe Close in Cumbria. It is thought that those of a rectangular plan may have been influenced by the building of forts and *vici*. Although some of these structures were built of stone, most were of timber, particularly in valley-locations. Stone was employed much more on upland sites, both because of availability and because of the relative scarcity of timber.

In areas where these sites have been related to their landscapes, those at lower level are characterised mostly by smaller fields, suitable for growing crops (or hay), whilst those at higher levels seem to have incorporated the larger enclosures associated with stock-management. The climatic environment certainly changed during the period of the Roman occupation; better conditions during the second and third centuries may have allowed a range of crops, including some viticulture, and grain-growing up to an altitude of approximately 350 metres. Deteriorating conditions in the fourth century undoubtedly compromised this ability. As we have seen, the northern farmer would expect to sell on his surplus to a nearby *vicus*, either in a processed state, or ready for processing in the *vicus*.

The populations of these zones were mixed: some no doubt derived from local roots, and perhaps occupied farms used by their families for generations. Some better quality land was requisitioned to provide the discharge-settlements for serving soldiers. It is evident that whilst no doubt some northern farmers had to eke out a living, others were prosperous, and thus able to stimulate trade in the *vici*. The point is proved by the fact that it was possible to 'recruit' for *civitas*-administration men who, like their southern counterparts, were wealthy enough to sustain such a role. Further, there is some evidence to suggest that despite a physically unpretentious 'estate-centre', some farms commanded many hundreds of acres of land.

The conclusion must be that, despite the very different faces presented by agriculture in the north and south of the province, both can be considered effective and profitable, drawing the farmers fully into the Romano-British economy, and as result into the culture of Romanisation. Roman Britain fully justifies the 'vibrant Britannia', depicted on a *sestertius* of the emperor, Antoninus Pius, and in practice showed itself capable of responding to the extensive economic demands made of it when, in the later fourth century, the province appears to have been cast in the role of an arsenal for the western empire. Calgacus' caricature retreated further and further from the reality.

6

The place of religion in Romano-British society

We have seen that through the shared work of administration and through the economics of supply and demand, a successful and integrated Romano–British society emerged. A powerful bonding-force to this society was provided by the wide variety of religious rituals practised within the province. Although in a few cases – most notably Christianity – the Roman state found itself at odds with a religious cult of provincial origin, the Romans were in general tolerant of the religious practices which they encountered in the empire, evidently believing that people were best left free to continue to seek the protection of their traditional gods.

Religious practices in Roman Britain fall into a number of groups. First, there were cults, such as Emperor-worship and the cult of Jupiter, which were effectively obligatory on Romanised communities. Second, the gods of the traditional Olympian pantheon, which consisted of deities with distinctive protective functions, were occasionally worshipped alone or, through the process of *interpretatio Romana*, in conjunction with their closest equivalents in the Celtic pantheons. Third, the cosmopolitan nature of Romano-British society saw the introduction of a wide range of so-called 'mystery' cults from various parts of the empire; these may have had a temporary political or social relevance, and generally appealed to rather restricted groups of people. Fourth, we should consider as a separate issue the progress of Christianity in Roman Britain. Whilst this, in a number of ways, resembled the mystery-cults, its most obvious distinction was that, whilst they were mostly tolerated by the authorities, it was not – until the early fourth century.

In the early imperial period, at least, ruler-worship was not officially countenanced in the west, although it was a natural feature of the culture of the Hellenistic Kingdoms of the east; there, from Augustus' time, emperors were hailed as gods and equated with various of the Olympians. In the west, although individual emperors may have had pretensions to personal divinity, the 'imperial cult' stopped short of such claims, and directed attention instead to the 'guardian-spirit' (*genius* or *numen*) of emperors. The observance of this was officially required, although it was in reality as much a political as a religious act – a statement of loyalty.

Units of the Roman army took an oath of allegiance to the emperor, which was renewed annually; each year fresh altars were inscribed affirming their continuing loyalty, and set up within military sites. Communities of Roman citizens had an obligation similar to that of the army, and individuals often had statuettes of emperors which they placed on their household altars; the manufacture of these, in bronze or terra cotta, will have represented a sizeable item of trade. Provinces had imperial-cult centres; altars stood at Lyons (*Lugdunum*) and Cologne (*Colonia Agrippinensis*), for example, whilst in Britain, the centre was the impressive temple erected in the classical style in the *colonia* at Colchester which, for a time at least, was regarded as the administrative 'capital' of Roman Britain. The temple was serviced by six priests (*Seviri Augustales*) and, as well as providing for the *colonia*, will once a year have been the centrepiece of a provincial gathering at which representatives of the *civitates* met.

It is known that the temple initially caused much resentment as land and money were appropriated for its construction and local people put to work on it. Because of this, this 'symbol of an alien domination' was, as we saw (see p.19), a particular target during Boudicca's rebellion; the altar to Victory, which stood outside it, was overturned, and a bronze head of Claudius which was recovered from the river Alde (in Suffolk) may have been looted from the temple and deposited in the river as an offering to a local deity, perhaps to demonstrate the superiority of the local god over the Roman 'Emperor-god'. In time, however, local people came to accept the ceremonial, and those who were wealthy competed for the opportunity to organise it; this was a way for those who desired it to bring themselves to notice, perhaps as a stepping-stone to a rising career in administration. The calendar of the imperial cult may have become relatively full, with birthdays and anniversaries of the emperor and members of his family, and of some emperors who had merited the accolade of posthumous deification.

It was not uncommon for activities which had no direct connection with the imperial cult to be linked with it as a way for communities and groups to demonstrate their loyalty. Thus, the theatre at Brough-on-Humber was dedicated during the reign of Antoninus Pius in honour of the 'Divine House', whilst the townspeople of Vindolanda linked a dedication to Vulcan (the 'smith-god') with a prayer for the safety of the 'Divine House'. In this way a sense of political loyalty can be seen to have been all-pervasive.

Just as significant as a focal point for loyalty to Rome was the cult of Jupiter, usually styled 'the Greatest and Best' (*Jupiter Optimus Maximus*, or *IOM*). Jupiter, too, will have figured amongst the annual oaths of members of the Roman army, and his altars kept in the 'chapels' which were part of the headquarters of Roman forts. These were replaced each year, and the redundant altars were ceremonially buried – the source of the fine collection associated with the fort at Maryport (Cumbria). Jupiter also occupied a significant role for civilians, and it is likely that the market-squares (*fora*) of *civitas*-capitals had as dominant features a column with a Corinthian capital decorated with heads of Jupiter. It seems likely that the 'Jupiter-capital' from Cirencester occupied such a prominent position. Jupiter's role will have assumed an added significance when the emperor, Diocletian, adopted the title *Iovius* ('Jupiter's own').

Jupiter, as head of the Roman pantheon, probably remained rather special and official; the other Olympians, however, penetrated much more obviously into the everyday life of the Romano-British. These gods were viewed as presiding over activities, connected with civic life, security, work, prosperity, domestic life or leisure-activities, and were acknowledged either on their own or in parallel with a close equivalent from local pantheons. Thus, Mars-Camulos is found at Colchester, and Mars-Ocelus at Carlisle; in both cases, the Roman god of war has been 'paired' with a local equivalent.

In many cases, these Roman or Romano-Celtic deities presided over functions which were presumably important to the life of groups or communities. As we have seen (see p.52), the people of Vindolanda made a dedication to Vulcan, the 'smith-god', indicating that the town regarded its manufacturing relationship with the adjacent fort as a principal source of prosperity. Similarly, Corbridge has produced evidence of a plaque showing what is evidently a Celtic deity who had properties similar to those of Vulcan; Corbridge, too, as a 'garrison-town' derived much of its prosperity from supplying garrisons on the frontier and from providing them with a repair-service. Apollo is frequently cited on inscriptions, often in conjunction with a local deity, such as Maponus; Apollo had concerns in both health and commerce, though a principal area may have been music. Presumably, the god was a patron to guilds of military musicians – a relief-carving of Apollo Maponus from Ribchester (Lancashire) depicts Apollo as the lyre-player (*citharoedus*), whilst a temple-site in the *vicus* at Papcastle (Cumbria) has produced a bronze statuette of the satyr-figure, Marsyas, who had the temerity to challenge the god of music to a contest and lost.

Members of the Roman army had their own favoured deities – some of them, such as Mithras, deriving from non-Roman origins. Of the classical deities, however, Mars (as the god of war) was obviously appropriate, sometimes in association with a relevant equivalent. Thus, as Housesteads (on Hadrian's Wall), a group of German soldiers put up an altar to Mars Thincsus; Thincsus was a Germano-Celtic counterpart to the Roman god of war. Another eminently suitable deity for members of the Roman army was Hercules – the god who laboured hard for the good of others; it is probably also significant that the army should favour a deity of considerable interest to a number of Roman emperors, some of whom appear to have seen themselves as the god's embodiment on earth. Alongside these deities, members of the Roman army also embraced a range of semi-divine personifications, such as Fortuna and Victoria.

Besides the Roman and Romano-Celtic deities, we find examples of Celtic deities in Romanised forms; thus, at Carrawburgh (on Hadrian's Wall), we find Coventina, who presided over a spring, depicted as a classical water-nymph. Near Lancaster, Julius Januarius, a retired cavalry-*decurion*, made a dedication to a god named Ialonus, who was almost certainly the deity of the river Lune; Januarius had evidently been settled on land in the river-valley, and needed the god's good-will to secure a successful harvest. Akin to such appeals for 'local divine protection' were the approaches made to a range of political or civic tutelary deities. From Birrens (Dumfriesshire) came a fine relief-carving of *Dea Brigantia*, the personified guardian of the tribe of the Brigantes; she appears in a fully Romanised form as a classical 'Winged-Victory'. Similarly, towns 'invented' their own guardians, who are often seen in the form of female personifications, wearing mural or gated crowns.

Although these deities were observed in private, as well as public, venues, their relevance to people was largely as part of communities or other – for example, professional – groups. In public, at least, the proliferation of such cults allowed for the performance by local people of priestly duties related to cult-temples. In many cases, such 'jobs' may well have been hereditary, as was probably the case with the Gaul, Julius Sacrovir – (the name means 'holy-man') – who raised the standard of rebellion against Rome in Gaul in AD 21. The priests' duties will have included the management of cult-calendars, no doubt defraying expenses where appropriate, and offering the necessary advice to those who sought it. In the case of a successful outcome, it was then the duty of those who sought the advice to carry out their part of the 'bargain', often the erection of an altar, recording the success, which ended with the formula, *VSLM* ('willingly and deservedly fulfilled his vow').

Although, as has been said, such gods dealt principally with groups and communities, there was room for private requests; an altar found in County Durham, for example, records the fulfilment by an army-commander of a vow to Silvanus (the 'forest-deity') in return for a successful outcome to a boar-hunt. Further, some sites, such as Uley in Gloucestershire, have revealed personal 'curses' (*defixiones*) inscribed on lead-sheet and fixed to temple-walls; these generally sought some form of retribution for a wrong done to the person making the curse.

Although many people will have had in their houses personal shrines to a variety of 'relevant' deities, the observance of the Romano–Celtic pantheons was largely a public matter. Temples were not, however, places for congregational worship; the temple was literally the 'house of god', in which the god's image was kept, to be 'consulted' by the priests of the cult. People seeking the advice of such gods gathered outside, around an altar-group, to hear the priests' pronouncements. Temples might, as for example at Trier in Germany, be located in a group, presumably in a religious area; or they might occupy specific holy places, as did the temple erected around the natural spring at Carrawburgh (on Hadrian's Wall), which was regarded as sacred to Coventina.

In a few cases, temples were executed in the classical style, as was the case with that of Sulis Minerva who presided over the healing waters at Bath. This site was clearly a focus for pilgrimage for a wide variety of people, who will have guaranteed the wealth and importance of the cult-centre. In most cases, however, gods' images were housed in Romano-Celtic temples: these were built after a pre-Roman 'design', but executed in materials and in a style which might be regarded as Romanised – for example, the use of stone and tile in preference to timber and thatch. The long pre-Roman history of such buildings was vividly demonstrated by a structure located in the 1940s during construction-work at Heathrow Airport, which dated back to c. 500 BC.

Such Romano-Celtic temples varied in size and shape; most were square or rectangular, though some were circular, polygonal or even triangular. The general configuration was a tall *cella* to be lit by a clerestory, and surrounded at a lower height by an ambulatory (or colonnade). Such a structure may be seen inside the great hillfort of the Durotriges at Maiden Castle (in Dorset), and within the remains of the Romano-British town at Caerwent (in Gwent), where the *cella* has a small apse, in which (presumably) the god's image stood (or sat). Inscriptions, of course, indicate the existence of a great many more such temples than have been located.

Although Romano-Celtic paganism came into increasing competition with a variety of other cults, mostly originating in the eastern part of the empire, it remained supported by some until very late in Romano-British history. Just as the observance of paganism remained relatively resilient in the fourth century amongst the administrative classes in Rome itself, so, in many provinces, highly-placed people were evidently hesitant to embrace new religions. In Britain, the point is made sharply by the construction in the second half of the fourth century of a extensive cult centre to Nodens (or Mars Nodens) at Lydney (on the Severn-estuary). As in Rome, much paganism was probably absorbed into local expressions of Christianity; such was the innate conservatism of the Romanised mind, which may have bordered upon the spirit of ecumenism.

As has been said, the chief significance of Romano-Celtic paganism was its role in binding the British into a Romanised culture. Ultimately, however, such cults, like the state religion of Rome, were materialistic; wealth and success were their objectives rather than moral improvement or spiritual satisfaction. For such needs as these, a variety of non-Roman cults, mostly from the eastern Mediterranean, became available – largely due to the cosmopolitan nature of the Roman army and of those engaging in trade and commerce. The nature of these so-called 'mystery-cults' was very different from that of Roman or Romano-Celtic paganism.

Some such cults must have had a very transitory presence in

Britain and are known from a small number of inscriptions erected by devotees. An example is the cult of Jupiter-Dolichenus, recorded, for instance, at Corbridge (in Northumberland) and Ribchester (in Lancashire), where soldiers or merchants must temporarily have established cult-centres; the god represents an assimilation between Jupiter (as head of the Roman pantheon) with the sky-deity from Doliche (in Syria). There may have often been a political dimension to expressions of interest in such cults, when they were known to have been favoured by members of the imperial family. This appears to have been a relevant consideration in the early years of the third century, which saw Septimius Severus and his imperial entourage based at York. Severus' wife, Julia Domna, was of Syrian origin; it is likely, therefore, that the cult of Jupiter-Dolichenus saw a temporary boost because of her presence in Britain. An inscription from York, which can be dated to *c.* AD 206, records the construction of a temple to the Egyptian god, Serapis; Severus himself was a known devotee of the Egyptian cults. Similarly, the popularity of sun-worship, another eastern cult, probably had its origin in imperial interest in it; one emperor, Aurelian (AD 270–275), even appears to have sought to put the Sun in Jupiter's place as the 'head' of the imperial pantheon.

These cults required a different kind of involvement from that appropriate to the state-paganism; many of them involved gods whose theology was concerned with the death and rebirth of nature; in this sense, they were fertility-figures, perhaps like the groups of three Mother-goddesses who were frequently commemorated, but in a 'sanitised' and widely-acceptable form. Gods who 'died' and who were then resurrected were seen to be taking the burdens of mankind upon their shoulders and thus suffering for them. The kind of relationship, therefore, which came about between god and devotee was personal and infinitely more spiritual than was ever the case with the 'official' gods. Whilst the great majority of these cults were tolerated by Rome, because they posed no obvious political threat, they did not generally form part of an official organisation or benefit from official sponsorship. For this reason, the numbers of devotees involved at any one time will have been relatively small.

The cult of the Persian god, Mithras, provides a reasonable illustration, and demonstrates a shared background with other eastern cults. Mithras was instructed by the sun to kill the sacred bull so that the bull's blood and semen would fall to earth to fertilise it. The task proved arduous, and the story of it contained at least one moment of self-doubt on Mithras' part which is reminiscent of the famous incident in the Passion of Christ in the Garden of Gethsemane. The successful completion of the task saw Mithras overcome his suffering, defeat the forces of darkness who wished to deny mankind the benefits which Mithras sought to bring, and thus stand as the guardian of light, prosperity, honesty and truth.

A number of Mithraic temples have been recognised in Roman Britain, most notably that outside the fort of Carrawburgh on Hadrian's Wall. These temples shed some light on Mithraic beliefs and practices, though a total picture is denied us because of the cult's secrecy. As elsewhere in the empire, the devotees of Mithras in Britain appear to have consisted principally of soldiers and merchants, who will presumably have been attracted by the cult's hierarchy, sense of comradeship and insistence on integrity. That it was in no sense, however, a 'soft option' seems clear from the relatively small size of most temples (holding perhaps 20 or 30 cult-members) and from what is known of the discipline involved in initial entry and in passage through the grades of the hierarchy. It also appears that the Mithraic sites were not occupied on a continuous basis, but in phases interspersed with periods of neglect – presumably as cult-members, and particularly those senior in the hierarchy, moved on. At Carrawburgh, for example, there were four periods of activity; of these, the first (in the second century) was very modest in size. There were then two separated phases in the third century, which showed an enlargement of the temple; a final phase (in the fourth century) appears to have come to a violent conclusion – presumably reflecting the current conflict between Mithraism and Christianity.

The temples were evidently windowless – to imitate the cave in which Mithras lived; that at Carrawburgh – and it appears similar to that which was found in 1952 at Walbrook (London) – consisted of an entrance which led into a small ante-chamber, which in its turn led into the 'chapel' itself. This ante-chamber may have been used for initiation-ceremonies. The 'chapel' consisted of a nave, flanked by two raised side-aisles, upon which were probably set benches for the initiates. The nave was guarded by the two 'attendants', Cautes and Cautopates (the Rising and the Setting Sun), who, with Mithras himself, represented the 'Mithraic Trinity' (three figures in one god). At the head of the nave, there will have been the gaudily painted relief-carving of Mithras slaying the bull. At Carrawburgh, this was fronted by altars, one of which carried a likeness of Mithras ('the unconquerable God') wearing the radiate crown of the sun, which was pierced through to allow passage of light from a lamp placed in a hollowed-out recess at the back of the altar. The Mithraeum at Housesteads also contained a carving of the birth ('hatching') of a fully-grown Mithras, complete with torch and dagger, from an egg of rock. The temple in London revealed a cache of fine sculpture, including a marble head of Mithras which is very reminiscent of Alexander the Great.

The conduct of ceremonial was probably very atmospheric: there was an absence of *natural* light, though in one Mithraeum (in Ostia), it appears that an *oculus* in the roof allowed the sun's rays to alight on the bull-slaying sculpture at midday. Artificial light was evidently, at some sites at least, controlled by being admitted through the pierced sun-ray crown around Mithras' head. Charred pine-cones found at many sites suggest their use as incense. Further, if Mithraic wall-paintings are to be trusted, the initiates wore bizarre dress to mark their grade in the cult's hierarchy.

Although the number of *known* Mithraic temples in Britain remains relatively small, finds of objects bearing a Mithraic meaning are sufficiently widespread to suggest that sites existed in the prox-imity of most military establishments, and in many towns which included in their populations both merchants and former soldiers.

It is evident that, by the fourth century, the rivalry between Mithraism and Christianity was strong: similarities in their rituals encouraged Christians to believe that Mithraism represented a form of Satanic mockery of their own beliefs. This sense will have been encouraged by the secrecy of practice in both cults – natural in the case of Mithraism, enforced in the case of Christianity, at least until Constantine's toleration in AD 312. As we have seen, this rivalry seems to have culminated in violent attacks launched by Christians upon Mithraic sites, including decapitation of statues, destruction of paraphernalia and defacing of decorations.

Mithraism was not at odds with the needs of the Roman state; indeed, from the third century AD, many emperors were devotees of the Sun and Mithras. Christianity, however, was not tolerated; the letters of the emperor, Trajan, written to the younger Pliny whilst the latter was the governor of Bithynia (in *c.* AD 112), shows that, although they were not to be hunted down, Christians were required ultimately to conform by their observance of the imperial cult. This, however, they were unable to do; thus a secret existence provided the only means for Christianity to survive. Also, Christians tended to be misunderstood and were, therefore, unpopular; they were picked out as scapegoats to take the blame for the Fire of Rome (in AD 64) because they were regarded as cannibals (an obvious reference to the Eucharist) and as anti-social (a reference to their exclusiveness). Their illegal status, for obvious reasons, drove Christians underground; as far as evidence is concerned, therefore, we can recognise their presence only through the interpretation – often far from conclusive – of small personal objects.

It would, of course, be a mistake to think that persecution went on all the time or that it was conducted uniformly across the empire. Persecution usually occurred when local or more widespread problems persuaded the local or central authorities of the need to divert blame on to other parties. In these circumstances, the 'rule', 'more Christians, more disasters' appears to have been regarded as providing a suitable one to pursue. The viciousness, however, with which persecution (when it occurred) was often activated could prove to be counter-productive; 'the blood of the martyrs,' announced Tertullian (in the early third century), 'is the seed of the Church'.

It is not clear when Christianity first made an appearance in Roman Britain, though there may have been merchants from other parts of the empire, who were converts themselves, coming to Britain even in the first century. It is generally recognised that the earliest dateable piece of material evidence is a fragment of amphora-wall, which carried part of a well-known cryptogram, which was probably of Christian significance which, when its letters are re-arranged, gives twice the words *Pater Noster* ('Our Father') arranged in a cross, with two 'spare' As and Os'; these signify *alpha* and *omega* ('the beginning' and 'the end'). This was found in a *vicus*-location at Manchester and dates from around the middle of the second century AD. It is, however, thought by some that the significance of this relates to the practice of magic rather than Christianity; indeed, double-meanings on supposedly Christian objects present difficulties. For example, do the words *anima mea* on a ring from Vindolanda mean 'my soul' (the opening words of the *Magnificat*) or 'my darling'?

It is, of course, clear from the incidence of diagnostic objects that the number of Christians was growing, though it is not possible to tell whether this was a speedy process, (as Tertullian and Origen appear to suggest in the third century), or what kind of organisation linked believers. Britain was clearly subject to some persecution; St Alban was martyred probably with Geta as his judge, when Septimius Severus and his entourage were in Britain in the first decade of the third century. Julius and Aaron may have been martyred at Caerwent during the persecution of Decius and Valerian in the mid-third century. Diocletian's persecution, however, hit the east of the empire hardest, and it is believed that in Britain Constantine's father, Constantius Chlorus, did no more than was absolutely necessary.

In terms of evidence, the situation does not become a great deal clearer even after Constantine's acceptance of Christianity; although some objects, such as tombstones, are more explicit in their references than would have been possible before and although some sites, such as the cemetery at Poundbury, give a clearer indication of Christian involvement, the organisation of the religion remains elusive. Such finds as the Water Newton plate provide evidence of wealth and status, but positively identified churches remain rare, and we are left with a degree of ambivalence over such structures as the so-called 'church' at Silchester, which looks almost as Mithraic as Christian. It is possible (though not yet proved) that churches with unique or rare dedications may conceal a Romano-British origin – such as that of St Elphin (Romano-British *Alphinus*) at Warrington.

That an organisation of some sort existed, however, is clear from the fact that British bishops attended famous Church-Councils in the fourth century – Arles in AD 324 and Rimini in AD 359; in the case of the latter, however, it is interesting that the British bishops needed financial help from Constantius II towards the outlay on the journey – unless this represented temporising by men who only a few years previously had probably supported the rebel, Magnentius, against Constantius.

If, however, this does indicate poverty on the Church's part, it seems inconsistent with the considerable evidence for wealth in the fourth century, at least in the Lowland zone; not only do the *Panegyrics* contain references to economic prosperity but a number of villas – for example, Lullingstone (Kent) and Hinton St Mary (Dorset) – have lavish interior decorations which clearly belonged to Christians; Lullingstone has a wall-decoration with figures in the 'praying mode', whilst Hinton St Mary has an extensive mosaic floor with the 'head of Christ' occupying its centre. Nor is there much to illuminate the relationship between Church and society, although a recently-discovered salt-pan from Cheshire bears an inscription which suggests a relationship over industrial ownership similar to that associated with medieval monasticism.

In all, therefore, the nature and role of the Christian Church in Roman Britain, even in the fourth century, remain ambiguous, with such evidence as there is pressed into service to support a number of often mutually exclusive conclusions. It may be that, situated as it was on the edge of empire, Roman Britain 'encouraged' a less structured Church organisation than was the case in other parts of the empire. In one respect, however, the influence of Christianity in the province may have been significant; Pelagius, who gave his name to the heresy of Pelagianism, was Romano-British. This heresy, with its belief that man was the master of his own salvation, well suited those of independent spirit, who tried at the turn of the fourth and fifth centuries to buttress Romano-British culture against the loss of the integrity of Britain as a structural part of the empire. This heresy was still sufficiently vigorous in AD 429 for St Germanus to come from Gaul in an effort to deal with it.

Thus, from the point of view of supplying the 'cement' which held Romano-British culture together, the official religions of Rome played a major part. It is an irony that Constantine's peace with the Church which was meant to bring to an end decades of divisiveness instead aided the fragmentation of the empire: it is equally ironic that it took a Christian heresy to provide the backbone which kept Romano-British culture alive at a time when it appeared to have little else to support it. And it was the Romano-Celtic Church in the west which allowed the Christianity that had come in the Roman period to survive the 'Dark Ages'.

7

The later years

For a long time it was taken as axiomatic that Roman Britain came to an end in AD 410; for those requiring precise dates, it appeared to suffice. It is now understood that the evidence upon which this was based – a reference in the late historian, Zosimus – had been incorrectly interpreted; the rescript of the emperor Honorius, giving instructions for the institution of local measures for self-defence, was addressed not to the Britons, but to the Bruttii of southern Italy. As a result, we not only lose a date but are provided with an opportunity to view the decline of *direct* Roman influence in Britain not as an event, but as a process, extending over a considerable period. Although the nature of archaeological evidence for the later fourth and fifth centuries does not always facilitate *precise* interpretations, it does allow us to glimpse important cultural transformations which were occurring during this period and which represent the reality of the 'end of Roman Britain'.

The processes which eventually put unstoppable pressures on the territorial integrity of the Roman empire were already underway at the turn of the second and third centuries, when Septimius Severus and his entourage were in Britain attempting to find a permanent solution to the problems of the northern frontier (see Chapter 3). Their work appears to have been successful to the extent that the northern frontier-area was peaceful for most of the third century; indeed, the linear-barrier itself probably fell into decay, and the manning-levels at some, at least, of the forts were probably allowed to fall. Just as significant was the decision, taken during the third century, to transform areas of northern Cumbria into the *civitas Carvetiorum*, with a *territorium* in the Solway Plain and Eden valley and a centre at Carlisle. Such demilitarisation indicates the prevalence of peace *and* prosperity, since local leaders will have needed to be wealthy enough to take on the burdens of local government; we may assume that this prosperity had sprung from lucrative contracts to supply the frontier-army.

Although Britain was probably less susceptible to the kind of population pressures which affected the European provinces, there clearly were, as time went on, growing anxieties concerning the activities of Picts (from the north), Saxons (from the east), and Scots (*Scotti*, from the west). Immediately, however, in the third century, the most pressing problems were those which were internal to the empire – the political 'muscle-flexing' of the army, anarchy and inflation. The state of the coinage is a clear measure of financial problems – particularly the demonetising of lower denominations and the introduction of new higher denominations; by the middle of the century, inflation was so serious that the official mints could not cope with the demand for coinage, and the consequent local copying produced huge numbers of 'barbarous radiates' of very poor quality. In such circumstances, we may assume that many people will have returned to a system of barter, as so many coins were needed to make the simplest of purchases.

Because of changes introduced by Septimius Severus, it had become much easier for ordinary soldiers to achieve promotion through the ranks to very senior positions; such was the origin of 'soldier-emperors' whose rise in the middle of the third century caused the anarchy which helped to fragment the empire. Between AD 260 and 273, Britain joined other western provinces in a breakaway movement known as *Imperium Galliarum* ('the empire of the Gauls'), which had its own emperors and other officials.

Clearly, the preoccupation with internal feuding in the empire meant that less attention was paid to matters of external defence and that more often than not people who were forced across the frontiers into Roman provinces were tolerated and allowed to settle. In Britain, there was certainly some Germanic settlement, although measures were put in hand to strengthen the south-east coast with some new forts, which in time developed into the system known as the 'Saxon shore'.

The rebellion in the west was brought to an end in AD 273 by the

71

emperor Aurelian (AD 270–275), who was himself followed by more stable rulers who began the business of imperial reconstruction. This process reached a significant stage with the accession of Diocletian in AD 284, whose changes as regards the administration of Britain have already been noticed (see Chapter 4). An effect of these in Britain, however, was to prompt another rebellion; Diocletian in a sense institutionalised the anarchy by splitting the empire into two, and appointing Maximian to control the western provinces. Carausius, evidently a naval commander in Gaul and Britain, took this as an invitation: he first of all declared himself the third emperor, issuing coins with the legend 'Carausius and his Brothers'. His 'brothers' (that is, Diocletian and Maximian) did not agree to share power with him, thus leaving Carausius as a rebel. He held power between AD 287 and 293 and was then murdered and succeeded by Allectus, who maintained his independence until his defeat by Constantius Chlorus in AD 296.

The value for Britain of this period of rebellion lay in the fact that attention was given to the specific defence needs of the province, particularly with regard to movement from Europe. Work on the Saxon shore continued with the first signs of a new military architecture, which appears to have been modelled upon town-walls in Gaul. The traditional Roman fort, with the shape of a playing-card, had effectively been a police-station, which housed men whose principal job had been located *outside* their forts. The new forts, such as Portchester, were equipped with high, thick walls and external bastions, which were presumably used for mounting pieces of heavy artillery. Their internal arrangements are often difficult to discern, but the forts themselves clearly played the part of defended strongpoints – that is, they were rather more akin to medieval castles, which to some extent they resembled. There was much difference between individual forts. Most were square or rectangular, though Pevensey took the shape of an irregular oval encompassing a small hill-top. Some had bastions all around their wall-circuits, whilst at others bastions were restricted to the corners; bastions were sometimes rounded and sometimes polygonal. Corners were now usually angular, rather than rounded. The lack of certainty with respect to internal arrangements makes it difficult to know how such forts were manned. Did they contain soldiers alone, or soldiers and civilians? What size of garrison did they contain? One suggestion is that the Legion II *Augusta* was based at Richborough and its troops deployed in small groups to the other forts of the Saxon-shore system. It must have been the intention of the system to repel, or at least to regulate, raiding; most raiders will probably have wanted to settle in Britain, since wanton vandalism was probably only seldom the motive behind the raiding.

It is often suggested that the second half of the third century represented a low ebb in the economic fortunes of Roman Britain; this is based particularly on the evident lack of upkeep in some towns and the appearance of cultivation within towns. It is likely that the economic crisis of the middle of the century and the subsequent efforts to correct it brought hardship in their train. Similarly, the walling of towns, which probably started at this time, will have been a substantial new financial burden on those responsible for their upkeep. Indeed, it has been suggested that Saxon settlers may have been put to work in the building of town-walls, receiving land inside the towns in return for this. Despite the attention paid to towns, there is no reason to believe that the important relationship between town and country-side deteriorated; indeed by early in the fourth century, imperial panegyrists were singing a song of British rural prosperity.

Diocletian's reforms of the empire's government and their application to Britain have been described above. In some senses – particularly with respect to internal changes in Britain – they probably introduced a welcome new feeling of stability, both in military defence and in civilian administration; the governmental changes themselves, however, were too rigid, and could not be maintained beyond the 'first generation'. Although Constantine I managed briefly to unify the empire's government, the fourth century saw a return to rivalry at the top, with a resurgence of difficulties for those trying to maintain territorial integrity in the provinces. At such a time, Britain plainly benefited from its position, and the first half of the fourth century probably witnessed the greatest material prosperity so far. Not only did some villas reach a previously unknown level of development and opulence but, less dramatically, some 'Iron-Age' farms appear to have become Romanised as 'cottage-farms' for the first time. Particular success appears to have attended the sheep-farmers of the west country; this manifested itself in the appointment of a procurator of weaving at Winchester, in large villas (such as at Chedworth and Woodchester) and in the phenomenal urban success of Cirencester. Not only this, but the loss of mining facilities at some sites on the Continent brought a new need for British resources; for example, tin-mining in Cornwall was resurrected after an apparent lapse during the earlier Roman period.

It appears that the closing years of the third century saw a renewal, after a considerable interval, of pressure on the northern frontier, in the shape of the Picts (from Scotland) and the *Scotti* (from Ireland). The threat appears to have brought Constantius Chlorus (the western *Caesar*) to Britain twice – in AD 296, when his principal concern was to return Britain to the control of the central government, and again, 10 years later. The defeat of the British rebellion of Carausius and Allectus is commemorated on the Arras medallion, which shows Constantius disembarking at London and receiving the homage of a personification of London; the legend proclaims him as 'The Restorer of Eternal Light'. Constantius may also on that occasion have set in train rebuilding work on the northern frontier.

It is evident that the rebuilding had to be radical in nature, because of the decay that had taken place during the third century. It is likely, too, that the rebuilding concentrated on the forts rather than on the linear barrier and the smaller installations; this appears to exemplify the new military imperative – defence in depth, in which enemies were not checked by a linear barrier, but ultimately turned by a succession of forts which would be encountered as they came south. The rebuilt forts show some changes from their pristine (Hadrianic) form: the regular facing pairs of barracks were replaced by so-called 'chalets', many of which were open-fronted, and with a variety of internal arrangements. This may signify different manning-arrangements; possibly the barracks were for irregulars rather than auxiliary units, and perhaps also they housed civilians from the *vici* as well. The logic of this presumably would have been that their security in undefended settlements could no longer be maintained. There is some evidence, too, that the defences of the Cumberland coast were reactivated on a selective basis, presumably to deal with a threat emanating from across the Irish Sea and to aid the protection of the harbour of *Moricambe* (Kirkbride). It is noticeable – though dating presents difficulties – that some blocking of gates occurred at refurbished forts; this occasionally affected complete gateways, but more often single carriageways. It is to be assumed that the purpose was to make the forts less penetrable, so that, like the forts of the Saxon shore, they could serve as defended strongpoints. Similarly, it has been suggested that, in some forts, former internal towers were strengthened to support artillery-pieces.

The difficulties of the west and north evidently did not subside; in *c*. AD 315, Constantine I assumed the title *Britannicus Maximus*, which presumably conveyed success in a British enterprise. During the following decade or so, the west coast saw a programme of construction of new forts, which followed a similar plan to those in the east, with high, thick walls and bastions. Such forts are seen at Cardiff, Caernarfon, Caer Gybi (Holyhead) and further north at Lancaster. It may also be significant that at Lydney (on the Severn estuary) and at Cockersands Moss (near Lancaster) we have evidence of the cult of the Irish deity, Nodens (or Mars Nodens), suggesting the possibility of Irish settlement in western coastal areas.

After Constantine's death in AD 337 there was a return to civil war, and this must, as often before, have offered encouragement to Rome's enemies. An indication of this is conveyed by the fact that Constans made a visit to Britain in AD 342; that this visit took place in winter suggests that the background to it was probably an emergency of some description. This may have been connected with the fact that the British provinces had supported Constans' brother, Constantine II, whom Constans had killed in the recent civil war; rebellion or a need to impose his authority may therefore have provided Constans with a reason for his visit. Alternatively, it may have been connected with events on the northern frontier, as the great disaster of AD 367 – the so-called 'conspiracy of the barbarians' – was probably less of a sudden, totally unforeseen, event than the culmination of intermittent difficulties. The 'conspiracy' consisted of joint action between all the enemies of Roman Britain – Picts, Saxons and Franks – and brought destruction to all over the province. A significant component this conspiracy was evidently the treachery of those who acted as 'scouts' (*areani*) in the outpost-forts of Hadrian's Wall. These units were disbanded, and the outpost-forts abandoned.

That this was a cataclysm of major proportions cannot be doubted; but Britain was considered to be of sufficient significance for Count Theodosius to be sent with a field-army to restore the situation; the restoration included widespread reconstruction of forts and towns. That Britain merited this attention may seem surprising, but an indication of the reason may be provided by the fact that in AD 359, following a disaster on the Rhine, some 900 transport-ships were requisitioned to go to Britain to bring back all the resources that were needed to put the Rhine-installations back into commission. It is evident that Britain's position as an 'offshore island' gave it the status of a kind of safe haven or even a centre of resources for the western empire.

Although the historian, Ammianus Marcellinus, implies that the destruction of AD 367 was widespread and indicates that repairs were urgently put in hand, it is more difficult to trace these events through the evidence of archaeology; such evidence does not permit the necessary degree of precision. Certainly there is plenty of evidence of construction and reconstruction after the 360s, and the incidence of the calcite-gritted pottery made at Crambeck (in east Yorkshire), and normally referred to as 'Huntcliff-ware' (after the watchtower of that name, on the Yorkshire coast), is a useful indicator. The evidence also suggests that we should spread 'late rebuilding' over a much longer period than is sometimes regarded as appropriate; some of it should be placed well into the fifth century or even beyond. Bede, for example, in his *Life of St Cuthbert*, indicates that when Cuthbert visited Carlisle in the 680s, he found a Roman fountain still in working order. By contrast, we can point to some buildings which were not kept up and were in disrepair prior to AD 400, and others which were put to different uses from those originally intended. In other words, we have to be prepared to be flexible in an interpretation of 'late' Roman structures in Britain.

It is, however, generally assumed that Theodosius was responsible for the construction of a new (or partly new) series of watchtowers on the east coast. These were substantial constructions in the new military architecture and probably had the task of liaising with swift intelligence-gathering vessels (called *pictae*), which operated in the North Sea. These towers, of which five are known, possibly stretched from Filey to the Tyne estuary and were presumably in contact with the legionary fortress at York. There is a possibility that the west coast received similar attention; towers dated to the fourth century are known on the road running south from Carlisle and, as we have seen, some at least of the elements of the Hadrianic coastal system appear to have been put back into operation. It is also likely that, following the disaster of AD 367 some elements at least of the northern frontier were repaired and returned to use; in the late fourth century, some forts of Hadrian's Wall and some of the west coast exhibit a similar mode of construction. If the relevant section of the *Notitia Dignitatum* dates also to this period, then it is a reasonable supposition that for a time, at least, after AD 367, the strategy of 'defence-in-depth' was still in use.

As we have seen, it was at about this time that the name, *Valentia*, appeared: some have interpreted it as indicating the formation of a fifth province in Britain, though a more likely explanation is that is was an honorific title applied to the whole of Britain in recognition of the post-367 recovery, and derived from the current imperial nomenclature (*Valentinian* I).

The organisation of the army in Roman Britain in the last decades of the fourth century is difficult to determine, as much of the evidence is imprecise. There is some indication that on the northern frontier, at least, forts may have become more like fortified villages, and the units of the army stationed in them akin to farmer militias. It is in any case quite unclear at what strength any of the units which are mentioned in the evidence were maintained; nor can we have any certainty regarding the nature and origins of the solders involved. Yet the mere arrival from the mints of western Europe of coinage until *c.* AD 400 shows that the army was still receiving pay; this presupposes a surviving organisation. It is possible that the two separate commands given earlier in the century for Britain – those of the *Dux Britanniarum* and the *Comes Litoris Saxonici* – may have been amalgamated under a new officer, the *Comes Britanniarum*. Ironically, another indication of some surviving organisation is the continuing military anarchy in the empire, since in the 380s Magnus Maximus left Britain to make a bid for more substantial control in Gaul. Although defeated and killed in AD 388, Maximus may have been sufficiently strong to provide a temporary coherence amongst Roman troops in Britain; the locations of finds of his coins suggest that his chief strength was in the north and that he may have taken the struggle against the Picts into Scotland itself. A decade or so later, continuing military problems in Britain necessitated the sending of a field-army under Honorius' general, Stilicho. It is nonetheless difficult to determine the level and location of Stilicho's activities, even though a fragment of roof-tile, which was long assumed to provide evidence of Stilicho's building activities at Pevensey, has now been eliminated as a forgery of the twentieth century!

Any dilution of military effectiveness will not only have left Britain more vulnerable to its external enemies but also have adversely affected stability and communications in the countryside. Except in a few areas, it is likely that the objective of farming may have been reduced to self-sufficiency. A decline in rural prosperity and quality of life is indicated in some villas by a reduction in the number of rooms in use and the conversion of earlier living-rooms to more practical purposes. The effect of rural decline on the towns will have been severe, though probably patchy. Whilst, as we have seen, there is still evidence of urban repair and even of fresh building, the loss of agricultural prosperity had a corresponding effect in the towns; trade declined, and with it the general level of activity. There was less money to invest in development and refurbishment, and much of what money there was was probably devoted to an attempt to maintain the defensive circuits of town-walls.

There must have been considerable additions to the population of Roman Britain as 'raiders' settled (as is shown by the appearance of sunken houses, or *grubenhausen*), nonetheless there seems to have remained an overwhelming desire to defend the Romano-British culture. After three and a half centuries of occupation, the polarisation of 'natives' and 'occupiers' was long dead, and all were integrated in their Romano-British identity.

The defence of this appears to have taken two rather different forms: some wished to maintain an institutional link with the empire's centre, with Roman officials operating through the leaders of the *civitates*. The interest of these was in the *status quo*, despite the obvious fact that this could not provide a long-term option. Zosimus provides evidence of conflict in the closing years of the fourth and the early fifth centuries, when he writes of other groups who drove out their Roman officials. This has been widely assumed to provide evidence of hostility to Roman culture – as if Romanisation was only a thin veneer over a Celtic identity. More recently an alternative suggestion has been made. In the late fourth century a Romano-Briton gave his name to a Christian heresy – Pelagianism (see Chapter 6). The principal tenet of the heresy was to deny the act of Divine Grace and to argue that man was the master of his own salvation. Translated into the contemporary military and political realities of Roman Britain, this heresy was an indication of the independence of thinking of men who were prepared to defend their Romano-British identity by their own vigorous actions. They drove out those who were waiting for Rome to defend them and assumed the initiative for this themselves. Importantly, the desire to defend Romano-British culture was as great on the part of those who were being attacked. The evidence points to localised success on the part of both of these groups with their different methods: the local success of the *civitas*-leaders in St Albans is shown by St Germanus' visit to Britain in AD 429 in an effort to deal with Pelagianism. Similarly, the influence of such men can be seen in the continuation of some kind of Romanised life at Cirencester into the fifth century, and their organisation of the defence of the community using the site of the amphitheatre just outside the town-walls. At Wroxeter, archaeology has shown attempts to keep the baths – *basilica* – building in some kind of repair, again well into the fifth century, although the re-occupation of the hill-fort site at the Wrekin may indicate that ultimately the more militarily minded members of the community had their way. We have noted, too, the long-term survival of features of the Roman townscape at Carlisle.

Names such as Vortigern ('mighty leader') and Arthur ('bear-man') indicate that the more spirited Romano-British survivors fought to defend their heritage; the 'fort-villages' of the north may have provided centres for such activity. However, although the formal power of Rome had gone by the early part of the fifth century – the time at which the watchtowers of the Yorkshire coast ceased to operate – the individualistic efforts of the Romano-British within or without their Romanised centres demonstrated that in the minds of most the Roman peace was, despite increasing difficulties and growing desperation, worth the effort to defend it. In the minds of the late Romano-British, the Roman occupation of Britain was not to be dismissed as a passing interlude.

Appendix I: Dates

Selective list of Romano-British dates

55–54 BC	Incursions of Julius Caesar
AD 43	Invasion of Britain; annexation of the south-east
60–61	Rebellion of Boudicca
c. 60–69	Increasing restlessness in the north; Roman intervention required
69	Roman civil war; breakdown of the treaty with Cartimandua
71–74	Annexation of the Brigantes by Cerialis and Agricola
77–83	Governorship of Agricola; annexation of Scotland
87	Withdrawal of a legion from Britain; evacuation of Scotland and development of Stanegate frontier; consolidation of occupation in north-west England
c. 110–120	Disturbances in northern Britain (?); further withdrawals of Roman troops (?)
118–119	Victories won under Pompeius Falco
121–122	Hadrian's visit to Britain; start of work on Hadrian's Wall and the coastal system

c. 125	Inception of 'fort phase' on Hadrian's Wall (completed by *c.* 138)
143	Renewed invasion of Scotland; building of the Antonine Wall
c. 157	Break in occupation of the Antonine Wall, followed by selective re-occupation
c. 163	Abandonment of the Antonine Wall; re-occupation of Hadrian's Wall and the coastal system. Evidence of instability in the north
180	Governorship of Ulpius Marcellus; disturbances in the north
192	Death of the emperor, Commodus; renewed political instability; eventual emergence of Septimius Severus (197)
209–211	Severus in Britain; campaigns in northern Scotland, leading to an 'accommodation' with the Scottish tribes
c. 250	Beginning of fortification of the east coast
259–273	'Independent empire of the Gauls'; establishment of *civitas* of the Carvetii (?)
287–296	Rebellion in Britain of Carausius and Allectus
c. 306	Refurbishment of northern sites against hostilities from Scotland
c. 330–340	West-coast defences put in hand; increasing instability in the north
351–353	Rebellion of Magnentius
367	'Conspiracy of the barbarians'; followed by refurbishment of many northern sites and inception of watchtowers on the Yorkshire coast
383–388	Rebellion of Magnus Maximus; instability on all frontiers
c. 395	Stilicho in Britain
c. 400	Gradual fragmentation of order and administration

Selective list of Roman emperors

31 BC–AD 14	Augustus
AD 14–37	Tiberius

37–41	Gaius (Caligula)
41–54	Claudius
54–68	Nero
68–69 (Jan)	Galba
69 (Jan–April)	Otho
69 (April–Dec)	Vitellius
69–79	Vespasian
79–81	Titus
81–96	Domitian
96–117	Trajan
117–138	Hadrian
138–161	Antoninus Pius
161–180	Marcus Aurelius (jointly with Lucius Verus, AD 161–169)
180–192	Commodus
192–193	Pertinax
193	Didius Julianus
193–194	Pescennius Niger
193–197	Clodius Albinus
193–211	Septimius Severus
198–217	Caracalla
209–212	Geta
218–222	Elagabalus
222–235	Severus Alexander
238–244	Gordian III
244–249	Philip I
249–251	Trajan Decius
253–259	Valerian
253–268	Gallienus
268–270	Claudius II
259–273	'Independent Empire of the Gauls'
	Postumus 259–268
	Victorinus 269–271
	Tetricus I and II 271–273
270–275	Aurelian
284–305	Diocletian
286–308	Maximian
287–296	'British Rebellion'
	Carausius 287–293
	Allectus 293–296
293–306	Constantius I

306–337	Constantine I
337–340	Constantine II
337–350	Constans
337–361	Constantius II
351–353	Magnentius
360–363	Julian
364–375	Valentinian I
364–378	Valens
367–383	Gratian
375–392	Valentinian II
379–395	Theodosius I
383–388	Magnus Maximus
392–394	Eugenius
395–423	Honorius

Selective list of Roman governors of Britain

AD 43–47	Aulus Plautius
47–52	Ostorius Scapula
52–58	Didius Gallus
58–59	Quintus Veranius
59–61	Suetonius Paullinus
61–63	Petronius Turpilianus
63–69	Trebellius Maximus
69–71	Vettius Bolanus
71–74	Petillius Cerialis
74–77	Julius Frontinus
77–83	Julius Agricola
83–101	Sallustius Lucullus
	Metilius Nepos
	Avidius Quietus
101–?	Neratius Marcellus
115–118	Atilius Bradua
118–122	Pompeius Falco
122–125	Platorius Nepos
131–134	Julius Severus
134–138	Mummius Sisenna
138–145	Lollius Urbicus
155–158	Julius Verus
161–163	Statius Priscus
163–166	Calpurnius Agricola

175–178	Antistius Adventus
180–185	Ulpius Marcellus
185–187	Helvius Pertinax
191–196	Clodius Albinus
197–202	Virius Lupus
202–205	Valerius Pudens
205–207	Alfenus Senecio

Appendix II: Sources of information on Roman Britain

The classical sources

A great many men wrote historical works under the Roman emperors; some of these comprised chronological accounts of particular periods, such as Tacitus' *Histories* (AD 69–96) and his *Annals* (AD 14–68). Others, such as Suetonius, wrote *Lives* or biographies, which generally did not accept a chronological framework, but treated their subjects by themes. Most of what was written in antiquity has, of course, perished without trace, though it was undoubtedly used by those writers whose works have survived. We are left, however, with a problem of source-evaluation, for Roman writers seldom do more than to allude to their sources, usually without naming them.

We have to appreciate that the Romans had no knowledge of what today we should regard as historiography. In the first place, most 'writing' was done initially for a listening audience who would be expecting, to a large degree, to be entertained by what they heard. It is clear that at least some of what was produced was dismissed as 'boring', and that may have been because authors were straining too hard to impress with 'verbal fireworks', and were rather short on substance. Second, there was a tendency to see most motivation as inspired by character, and to view character as essentially immutable and only *revealed* by events.

The political atmosphere was also seen as a drawback; some emperors were both suspicious and repressive; they tended to lead to contemporary writers being unduly sycophantic during emperors' lifetimes and boldly and excessively critical after their deaths. There was also a problem with the flow of information; many decisions were taken by emperors within their own small circles of advisers whose deliberations might be the subjects of rumour, but rarely of fact. Further, many, though not all, writers were themselves active or retired politicians and administrators who might entertain a very subjective view of events, or even be trying to salve a bad conscience.

A final point to bear in mind is that Britain was a long way from the centre of the empire, and not a subject of vast concern to many Romans who might not be particularly interested in disentangling fact from fiction, and who would have little concern about the *minutiae* of places where frontiers and forts were established, or of details of landscapes against which battles were fought. To a Roman audience, a far-off province, such as Britain, assumed an importance if its governor or armies were main players on the imperial scene. Questions of morale, of bravery or cowardice, of leadership and heroism – these would be the chief points of identification between audience and subject-matter. Most battle-scenes cannot now be placed securely, and campaign-routes can only occasionally be elucidated; the oral nature of 'publication' gave no scope for explanatory maps, diagrams and footnotes. The kind of material requiring such elucidation was, therefore, omitted.

Thus, rather than the archaeologist turning for help to Roman writers, more often than not students of Roman historiography turn to the work of archaeology to help them understand the accounts of Roman Britain left by Roman writers.

The chief surviving writers

Publius Cornelius **Tacitus** (*c.* AD 55–120): Tacitus originated probably from Belgic Gaul, and was the first generation of his family to enter the senate; the fact that he was chosen as the son-in-law of Gnaeus Julius Agricola (governor of Britain, AD 77–83) is indicative of his promise; he reached the consulship in AD 97 after moving through the senatorial career under all the Flavian emperors. He became proconsul of Asia in *c.* AD 112. Most of his writing came after his consulship; his biography of his father-in-law, Agricola, and a treatise on the tribes of Germany were published in AD 98; his *Histories*, covering the period, AD 69–96 (though now largely lost), was published in *c.* AD 106, and some 10 or so years later came the

Annals. This covered the period AD 14–68, though portions of it, including the account of Claudius' invasion of Britain in AD 43, are lost.

Gaius **Suetonius** Tranquillus (*c.* AD 70–140): Suetonius was a school-master by profession and a member of Rome's second social order, the equestrians; he rose to senior administrative office in the service of emperors under Trajan and Hadrian, reaching the imperial secretariat, which gave him access to a wealth of imperial letters and papers. He was sacked in *c.* AD 122 apparently after some indiscretion, and never regained office. By nature a compiler of information and curiosities, he wrote a large amount, of which the most complete is now his *Lives of the Caesars*, biographies of the first 12 emperors from Julius Caesar to Domitian. These contain some information about Britain, in so far as his subjects were involved in the conquest and occupation of the province.

Cassius **Dio** Cocceianus (*c.* AD 163–230): Dio was a Greek from Nicaea in the province of Bithynia; his father reached the consulship and went on to hold a number of provincial governorships. Dio followed his father into the senate, achieving the rare distinction of holding two consulships – in *c.* AD 205 and in 229, with the emperor, Severus Alexander, as his colleague. Although favoured by the Severans, Dio appears not to have entertained a high opinion of them. He remained active in administration between 200 and 230, and appears to have done the bulk of his writing between *c.* AD 211 and 229. He set out to write (in Greek) a history of Rome from the foundation of the city down to his own times; most of his account of the period from 68 BC to AD 46 survives intact, whilst much of the remainder is covered by the Byzantine epitomators.

When he can be directly compared with other writers, Dio is not outstandingly accurate, and has a penchant for good stories, particularly those that have a moral to point. He also tends to assume that constitutional and political practices of his own day were relevant to earlier periods. His greatest value lies in his account of events contemporary to himself.

Herodian (*c.* AD 170–250): Little is known about Herodian's life, though it seems safest to assume that, whatever his origins, he rose to equestrian status and saw service in the imperial administration. Various cities of origin have been canvassed, and of them Antioch (in

Syria) seems the most likely. His account covers the period from AD 180 (the accession of Commodus) to 238 (the accession of Gordian III); his work is generally regarded as less reliable than Dio's, but superior to those of the writers of the Augustan History – perhaps an effort to be accurate vitiated by a degree of ignorance and an inability to resist rhetorical embellishment. Like Suetonius, however, his job appears to have given him access to imperial documents, and if, as some suppose, his patron in Rome was a senator, then that may have opened further sources to him.

Writers of the *Augustan History*: Despite the title, the *Augustan History* is, in fact, a collection of imperial biographies compiled ostensibly by six different authors in the period of Diocletian and Constantine – Aelius Spartianus, Julius Capitolinus, Aelius Lampridius, Flavius Vopiscus, Vulcacius Gallicanus and Trebellius Pollio. However, the broad agreement amongst scholars is now that in fact this 'scenario' is an elaborate piece of deceit, perpetrated for unknown reasons, and that the *Augustan History* was the work of one author writing in the late fourth century. The work starts with the *Life of Hadrian* and continues down to the late third century; because there is no formal introduction, it is widely believed that a portion is missing from the beginning which contained *Lives* of Nerva and Trajan, and thus maintained a continuation from Suetonius. The *Lives* are of very variable quality, the later ones in particular being regarded as largely fictional or gathered together through extracts taken uncritically from other authors; it can be shown that in many cases, documents which purport to be quoted verbatim are totally fictional. However, in general the earlier *Lives* (down to the Severi) are regarded as achieving a higher standard than the later ones.

Ammianus Marcellinus (*c.* AD 330–395): Like Herodian, Ammianus was a Greek from Antioch in Syria; but, unlike Herodian, Ammianus (for whatever reason) preferred Rome, and wrote in Latin. His *History of Rome* started with the accession of Nerva in AD 96, perhaps indicating that Ammianus saw himself as the 'literary heir' of Tacitus. Certainly, one of his complaints about the Roman aristocracy of his own day was the fact that they preferred superficial imperial biographies to serious works of history. A little over half of Ammianus' *History* survives (Books 14–31), covering the period, AD 354–378; this shows the relatively short space that was devoted to the first two and a half centuries of the historian's brief. Most of the research was done

88

in the late 380s and early 390s, and the *History* was published in *c.* AD 392. Ammianus evidently saw Julian's reign as the climax of his work; Julian was for him the embodiment of all the greatest qualities of earlier emperors, and a man who held out a promise that Rome could return to a golden age of virtue, justice and territorial integrity. Julian's successors failed to deliver on the promise. Although some threads of his work are biographical, even autobiographical, Ammianus stands as a historian because, as for his historical predecessors, for him the public affairs of Rome were more important than the acts and fates of individual emperors.

Zosimus (*c.* AD 450–500): Zosimus was a Greek historian, of whom little is known; he wrote his *New History* to cover the period from Augustus to *c.* AD 410, devoting over half of the work to events of the fourth century. A pagan himself, he attributed the decline of Rome to the decline of paganism, criticising the prominent Christian emperors, such as Constantine I and Theodosius, and, like Ammianus, taking Julian as his chief hero; Zosimus enjoyed administrative posts, and thus had first-hand knowledge of the mechanics of government. He is regarded as chiefly important for his account of events in Britain at the turn of the fourth and fifth centuries, for which his main source appears to have been the histories (or memoirs) of Olympiodorus of Thebes (Egypt) whose work (now largely lost) covered the period from AD 407 to 425 in 22 books. Other Greek sources of Zosimus' account of earlier events are Dexippus of Athens (of the third century) and the fourth-century sophist, Eunapius of Sardis.

Such is the shortage of surviving ancient literature which covers the affairs of Roman Britain that various other individual references have to be pressed into service. The reliability of many of these cannot be tested, though since many of them are from the works of poets, we have to expect a certain degree of licence. Examples of such works are:

- the *Silvae* of Papinius Statius (writing in the late first century AD), which contain references to Britain in the period of civil war (AD 69–70);
- the *Satires* of Juvenal (writing in the early second century AD), which refer to the Brigantes and a chieftain of theirs, named Arviragus (*c.* AD 100);

- the *Latin Panegyrics* of fourth-century emperors, which in a number of references suggest Britain as a kind of paradise at that time;
- the *Consulship of Stilicho* of the court-poet, Claudian (writing in the early fifth century AD), who provides almost the only evidence of Stilicho's activities in Britain in the latest years of the fourth century.

Chief references

Caesar's incursions in 55 and 54 BC:
- Caesar, *Gallic War* IV: 20–28; V: 8–23
- Dio Cassius, Roman History XXX: 51–53; XL. 1–3

Caligula's 'abortive invasion' (AD 40):
- Suetonius, *Life of Caligula* 44–46
- Dio Cassius, *Roman History* LIX: 2

Claudius' Invasion (AD 43):
- Dio Cassius, *Roman History* LX: 19–23
- Suetonius, *Life of Claudius* 17; *Life of Vespasian* 4

The mid-first century AD:
- Tacitus, *Annals* XII: 31–40; XIV: 29–39
- Dio Cassius, *Roman History* LXII: 1–12

The Flavian period:
- Tacitus, *Life of Agricola*
- Dio Cassius, *Roman History* LXVI: 20

Hadrianic events:
- SHA, *Hadrian* 5: 2; 11: 2; 12: 6

The Antonine period:
- SHA, *Antoninus* 5: 4
- SHA, *Marcus* 8: 7–8; 22: 1
- SHA, *Commodus* 6: 2; 8: 4; 13: 5
- SHA, *Pertinax* 3, 5–10
- Dio Cassius, *Roman History* LXXIII: 8–9

The Severan period:
- SHA, *Clodius Albinus* 13: 4
- SHA, *Septimius Severus* 18–19; 23: 3
- Dio Cassius, *Roman History* LXXV: 5; LXXVI: 11–16; LXXVII: 1
- Herodian, *Roman History* II: 15; III: 6–7; III: 14–15

The fourth century and beyond:
- Ammianus Marcellinus, *Roman History* XX: 1; XXV1: 4; XXVII: 8; XXVIII: 3
- Zosimus, *Roman History* VI: 2–5

The coin evidence for Roman Britain

Roman coins of the imperial period were frequently used to communicate the emperors' views of contemporary events and to bring major successes to public attention. Since a number of policy initiatives in Britain enjoyed high-profile status, it is not surprising that they found expression on the coinage.

1 Claudius' invasion of Britain in AD 43 was depicted on *aurei* and *denarii* between AD 46 and 50. The coins show a triumphal arch, as set up in both Rome and Colchester, and bearing on the architrave the legend DE BRITAIN. The invasion was also commemorated on a silver *didrachm* from Caesarea (in Cappadocia); this coin showed Claudius riding in a quadriga over the legend DE BRITANNIS.

2 It has been argued that Agricola's victory over the Caledonians at *Mons Graupius* was celebrated on Domitian's coinage. A *sestertius* of AD 84 shows a cavalryman riding down a barbarian enemy, and the legend connects the event with Domitian's seventh imperial acclamation, which occurred around September, AD 84. The problem is that if the battle was in AD 83, then the salutation is too late; if, on the other hand, it was in AD 84, then the salutation would be too early. It is safest *not* to take the coin as referring to Agricola's victory.

3 Hadrian's accession in AD 117 came at a time of disturbance in Britain, which had to be dealt with as a matter of urgency. *Asses* of AD 119 and 120 show Britannia seated facing front and in the 'dejected' pose; her foot rests on a pile of stones which some

91

have taken as representative of Hadrian's Wall; the coins, however, are too early for that, but presumably commemorate a victory won by Q. Pompeius Falco.

4 Hadrian visited Britain *c.* AD 121–122; it is thought by some that an *aureus* of AD 120 showing a reclining river-goddess may herald that visit by referring to the river Tyne. It is also thought that *sestertii* and *asses* of AD 136, which have the legend BRITANNIA, and show the personification much as in the earlier 'victory' types, may commemorate the visit. Particularly referring to the visit is a *sestertius* of AD 136 commemorating Hadrian's arrival (ADVENTVI AVG BRITANNIAE); perhaps significantly there was no issue in Britain's case of a coin commemorating Hadrian as 'Restorer' (RESTITVTOR) of the visited province. The design on the reverse of the ADVENTVS-coin is of Hadrian sacrificing over an altar, and faced by *Britannia*. Finally, in these coins commemorating the visits, a series of AD 137 refers especially to Hadrian's connection with the provincial armies; the coins show Hadrian addressing troops (*adlocutio*) with variants of a legend, EXERCITVS BRITANNICVS.

5 A number of coins of Antoninus Pius' reign refer to Britain; a sign of the importance to Antoninus of the advance into Scotland is the fact that whole issues of AD 143 were devoted to Britannia, to Victory, to Jupiter, Mars and Hercules and to Antoninus' relations with his troops. Legends on coins of all denominations include IOVI VICTORI, BRITANNIA and DISCIPLINA AVG; prominent too, is Antoninus' imperial salutation and personifications of Victoria, in one case holding a shield inscribed with the letters, BRITAN. In all cases, Britain looks alert and prosperous.

6 In contrast is an *as* of AD 154–5, depicting a 'dejected' Britannia, with the legend BRITANNIA COS IIII S C. It is assumed that this represents an indication of trouble in the northern frontier-area in Antoninus' later years, which led to a temporary evacuation of the Antonine Wall.

7 Although Marcus Aureius did not overtly refer to events in Britain on his coinage, some have assumed that the re-issue by Marcus Aurelius and Lucius Verus of the LEG VI type of Marcus Antonius' legionary series of 32–1 BC was significant. Two legions bore the number, six – VICTRIX in Britain and FERRATA in the east.

8 Commodus took the title BRITANNICVS for the victories of Ulpius Marcellus in AD 181–4; coins were issued in AD 184–5 to commemorate the event; they show Britannia and Victoria on the reverse with the legends including BRITT, VICT BRIT and VIC BRIT; Commodus included BRIT in the imperial titulary on the obverse. Commemorative medallions were also struck at the beginning of AD 185 to publicise the event.

9 The presence in Britain between AD 209 and 211 of Septimius Severus and his family and entourage received large-scale publicity on the coinage issued in the names of Severus himself and of his sons, Caracalla and Geta. As was the case with Antoninus Pius, whole issues were devoted to themes of warfare, Britain and victory between AD 208 (the departure from Rome) and 211 (Severus' death in Britain). Gods are commemorated (particularly Jupiter and Mars), as is Victory (named VICTORIA BRITANNICA). Severus and his sons are also shown in various triumphant situations, and all three added BRIT to the imperial titulary on the obverse of the coins. It is also striking that the victories were considered to be of sufficient significance to be commemorated on Greek coins struck in Alexandria. Of particular interest in the interpretation of the events of these campaigns are the 'bridge'-coins of Caracalla, with the legend, TRAIECTVS.

10 Although, subsequently, Britain produced coins from the London mint (AD 287–324), and at various times in the later third and fourth centuries was flooded with locally-made irregular issues and 'enjoyed' emperors, such as Carausius and Allectus, who were based in Britain, there are few other specific references on the coinage to events in Britain. It is, of course, possible, that some of the imperial 'virtues' which are commemorated refer to Britain (for example, PAX). There is a possible reference on two *aurei* of Victorinus (the rebel emperor of the *Imperium Galliarum*, AD 269–71), in the form of commemorations of Legion XX *Valeria Victrix*.

Two coins of Carausius have unusual references – EXPECTATE VENI, showing Britannia welcoming Carausius, and GENIO BRITANNI. The rebellion of Carausius and Allectus was brought to an end in AD 296 by Constantius I, who commemorated the event on the famous Arras-medallion, which shows a mounted Constantius disembarking from a barge, being welcomed by a figure kneeling in suppliant fashion in front of the gates of

93

London. The legend is REDDITOR LVCIS AETERNAE ('Restorer of Eternal Light'), which had both political and religious connotations.

For matters relating to the sources of information for Roman Britain, see S. Ireland, *Roman Britain: A Sourcebook*, London: Croom Helm, 1986.

Appendix III: Further reading

Although, because of their complexity, the publication of complete excavation-reports of Romano-British sites is both slow and expensive, a rapid 'turn-over' of information is achieved through the annual reports published in the journal, *Britannia*, in a section entitled 'Roman Britain in xxxx'. (This was, before 1970, published in the *Journal of Roman Studies*.) More mature thinking is carried in the reports of conferences, which are frequently published in the large (and growing) series of *British Archaeological Reports*.

The nature of the material inevitably means that the conclusions of reports and books in this field can be rapidly superseded; thus a relevant and up-to-date bibliography is constantly changing.

General works

These contain, in varying formats, accounts of late Iron-Age society, Roman conquest and occupation, the development of a Romano-British society and economy, together with discussions of the interpretative problems of later Roman Britain:

S.S. Frere, *Britannia* (3rd edn.), London: Pimlico, 1987.
G.D.B. Jones and D. Mattingly, *An Atlas of Roman Britain*, London: Blackwell, 1990.
M. Millet, *Roman Britain*, London: Batsford, 1996.
P. Salway, *Roman Britain,* Oxford: Oxford University Press, 1981.

H.H. Scullard, *Roman Britain,* London: Thames and Hudson, 1979.

M. Todd, *Roman Britain, 55 BC–AD 400* (3rd edn.), London: Fontana, 1997.

J.S. Wacher, *Roman Britain,* London: Dent, 1978.

A two-volume history is provided by:

J.S. Wacher, *The Coming of Rome,* London: Routledge, 1979.

A.S. Johnson, *Later Roman Britain,* London: Routledge, 1980.

A useful (though now old) guide to archaeological evidence is contained in:

R.G. Collingwood and I.A. Richmond, *The Archaeology of Roman Britain,* London: Methuen, 1969.

Aspects of conquest

G. de la Bédoyère, *Roman Towns in Britain,* London: Batsford, 1992.

G. de la Bédoyère, *Roman Villas and the Countryside,* London: Batsford, 1993.

D.J. Breeze, *The Northern Frontiers of Roman Britain,* London: Batsford, 1982.

D.J. Breeze and B. Dobson, *Hadrian's Wall* (3rd edn.), London: Penguin Books, 1987.

P.J. Casey, *Carausius and Allectus: The British Usurpers,* London: Batsford, 1994.

A.S.E. Cleary, *The Ending of Roman Britain,* London: Batsford, 1989.

W.S. Hanson, *Agricola and the Conquest of the North,* London: Batsford, 1987.

W.S. Hanson and G.S. Maxwell, *The Antonine Wall, Rome's North-West Frontier,* Edinburgh: Edinburgh University Press, 1983.

N.J. Higham, *The Northern Counties to AD 1000,* London: Longman, 1986.

P. Holder, *The Roman Army in Britain,* London: Batsford, 1982.

A.S. Johnson, *The Roman Forts of the Saxon Shore,* London: Elek, 1976.

G.S. Maxwell, *The Romans in Scotland,* Edinburgh: James Thin, 1989.

G.S. Maxwell, *A Battle Lost,* Edinburgh: Edinburgh University Press, 1990.

V.E. Nash-Williams, *The Roman Frontier in Wales* (2nd edn.), Cardiff: University of Wales Press, 1969.

D.C.A. Shotter, *The Roman Frontier in Britain,* Preston: Carnegie Publishing, 1996.

G. Webster, *Boudica,* London: Batsford, 1978.

The Romanisation of Britain

A.R. Birley, *The People of Roman Britain,* London: Batsford, 1979.

B. Cunliffe, *Fishbourne,* London: Thames and Hudson, 1971.

B.R. Hartley and L. Fitts, *The Brigantes,* Gloucester: Allan Sutton, 1988.

M. Henig, *Religion in Roman Britain,* London: Batsford, 1984.

N.J. Higham and G.D.B. Jones, *The Carvetii,* Gloucester: Allan Sutton, 1985.

M. Millet, *The Romanisation of Britain*, Cambridge: Cambridge University Press, 1990.

J. Percival, *The Roman Villa*, London: Batsford, 1976.

J.S. Wacher, *The Towns of Roman Britain*, London: Batsford, 1974.

D. Watts, *Christians and Pagans in Roman Britain,* London: Routledge, 1990.

G. Webster, *The British Celts and Their Gods under Rome*, London: Batsford, 1986.

C.R. Whittaker, *The Frontiers of the Roman Empire*, Baltimore: Johns Hopkins University Press, 1994.

Inevitably, with the pace of new discoveries and consequent re-evaluations, the state of our understanding of Roman Britain does not stand still, and books rapidly go out of date unless, like Frere's *Britannia*, they are periodically revised. Of the general works, Salway's *Roman Britain* (in the Oxford *History of England* series) and Frere's *Britannia* provide the most comprehensive accounts. Most recent is Millet's *Roman Britain*, which takes account of new directions in research. Most of the general books follow a similar format, recounting the military history and then dealing with the Romanisation of Britain in a series of topic-essays. However, Todd's *Roman Britain, 55 BC–AD 400* integrates both approaches. An excellent background is provided by both Wacher's *The Coming of Rome* and Johnson's *Later Roman Britain*; the latter in particular provides perceptive insights into a period where clarity is hard to achieve.

Archaeology has over the years grappled with a range of chronological and other questions regarding aspects of the military conquest and occupation; many of these remain very much open to question, few more so than the events of Agricola's governship (AD 77–83). Hanson's *Agricola and the Conquest of the North* provides a clear and thought-provoking account in the light of the more recent evidence, while Maxwell's *A Battle Lost* concentrates on the most intractable of all Agricolan problems – the location and significance of the general's final battle at *Mons Graupius*. New books on the frontiers are frequent, though Breeze and Dobson's *Hadrian's Wall* and Hanson and Maxwell's *The Antonine Wall* remain the standard treatments. Whittaker's *The Frontiers of the Roman Empire* sets the British frontier in a wider imperial context. Higham's *The Northern Counties to AD 1000*, as the title suggests, sets out to place the Roman conquest and occupation in a much broader than normal chronological context. The archaeological techniques deployed in the search for certainty are conveniently reviewed in Collingswood and Richmond's *The Archaeology of Roman Britain.*

In recent years, there has been a significant swing away from purely military pre-occupations towards the study of how the British adapted to becoming part of the Roman empire. Research on specific aspects, such as town and country, has produced various dedicated studies, but one of the most provocative books on the *whole* subject is Millett's *The Romanisation of Britain.* As stated above, those students who wish to pursue particular sites can turn to such series as *British Archaeological Reports* or the Monographs of the Society of Antiquaries of London (amongst many others); a short digest, however, of the most up-to-date material is contained in the annual reports contained in *Britannia,* a journal published by the Society for the Promotion of Roman Studies.